"Written by one of the most creative thinkers
about ADD and ADHD."

—Michael H. Popkin, Ph.D., author,
*Doc Pop's 52 Weeks of Active Parenting:
Proven Ways to Build a Healthy and Happy Family*

D0039941

# The
# Survival Guide
# for Kids with
# ADD or ADHD

## John F. Taylor, Ph.D.

free spirit
PUBLISHING®

**Library of Congress Cataloging-in-Publication Data**
Taylor, John F., 1944–
    The survival guide for kids with ADD or ADHD / John F. Taylor.
        p. cm.
    Includes index.
    ISBN-13: 978-1-57542-195-7
    ISBN-10: 1-57542-195-X
    1. Attention-deficit-disordered children. 2. Attention-deficit hyperactivity disorder.
    I. Title.
RJ506.H9T387 2006
618.92'8589—dc22                                                    2005033737

At the time of this book's publication, all facts and figures cited are the most current available. All telephone numbers, addresses, and Web site URLs are accurate and active; all publications, organizations, Web sites, and other resources exist as described in this book; and all have been verified as of October 2008. The author and Free Spirit Publishing make no warranty or guarantee concerning the information and materials given out by organizations or content found at Web sites, and we are not responsible for any changes that occur after this book's publication. If you find an error or believe that a resource listed here is not as described, please contact Free Spirit Publishing. Parents, teachers, and other adults: We strongly urge you to monitor children's use of the Internet.

The concepts, ideas, procedures, and suggestions contained in this book are not intended as a substitute for professional help.

Edited by Douglas J. Fehlen
Illustrated by Tad Herr
Cover design by Marieka Heinlen
Interior design by Percolator

 **Printed on recycled paper**
including 30%
post-consumer waste

10  9  8  7  6  5
Printed in the United States of America
S18860109

**Free Spirit Publishing Inc.**
217 Fifth Avenue North, Suite 200
Minneapolis, MN 55401-1299
(612) 338-2068
help4kids@freespirit.com
www.freespirit.com

## Dedication

Dedicated to the children for whom this book was carefully designed and written, and to their parents and siblings, all of whom have been challenged greatly by this powerful condition.

## Acknowledgments

I wish to give grateful acknowledgment to Douglas Fehlen of the editorial staff at Free Spirit for his patient and thorough editing. I also want to acknowledge my dear wife Jeanie for the innumerable ways in which she has provided support and encouragement throughout the development of this book.

# CONTENTS

## CHAPTER 8: EIGHT WAYS TO DEAL WITH STRONG FEELINGS

## LIST OF REPRODUCIBLE PAGES

# A Note on the ADD and ADHD Labels

This book can help you if you have been labeled **ADD.** ADD stands for **attention deficit disorder.** This book is also for if you have been labeled **ADHD.** ADHD stands for **attention deficit hyperactivity disorder.** Kids are given the ADD and ADHD labels because differences in the way their brains work make it hard for them to do some things—like pay attention or sit still.

Regardless of which label you have been given, *The Survival Guide for Kids with ADD or ADHD* can help you. The book uses the ADHD label because it's the one that most people who work with kids use. You can read more about these labels in Chapter 1. For now, you can remember that this book uses the label ADHD.

# Introduction

- Is getting ready for school a challenge for you?

- Do you have trouble paying attention at school?

- Is it difficult for you to sit still or stay in one place?

- Do you struggle to keep your things organized?

- Is it hard for you to control your anger?

- Do you sometimes have trouble making friends or getting along with others?

- Is it hard for you to fall asleep at night?

If you answered **YES** to any of these questions, read on!

# How This Book Can Help You

You can read more about words in **bold** type in the glossary on pages 108-110.

This book can help you if you have been labeled **ADHD.** ADHD stands for **attention deficit hyperactivity disorder.**

If you've been labeled ADHD, you probably face some challenges other kids do not. You might struggle at school—with paying attention to your teacher or focusing on the work you're supposed to do. It may be hard for you to learn some things that seem easy for other students. Or maybe you understand most of your work, but you have trouble staying organized. You might lose assignments or forget to hand them in. If ADHD makes it hard for you to sit still, teachers may get upset with your behavior. Sometimes it might seem as though you can't do anything right at school!

# Here are some things kids say about having ADHD:

"It's hard for me to pay attention. I often daydream or zone out."

"I can't slow down. It's like having a motor inside me that will not stop."

Having ADHD *can* be a real challenge . . . and not only when it comes to schoolwork and teachers. ADHD affects how you get along with other people, too. Maybe things don't always go smoothly with your parents or other family members at home. You might also have trouble making friends or getting along with other kids. It can seem as if *someone* is *always* angry with you.

ADHD can also create strong feelings inside you—like anger and sadness. It can affect your daily routines, how well you sleep, how you think about yourself, and even what you like to eat! One thing's for sure: Being a kid with ADHD isn't always easy.

Reading this book can help. It probably won't end *all* of the challenges you face, but you can use the ideas in it to manage your ADHD better in school, at home, and with friends.

Kids live in all kinds of families. When you read about *parents* in this book, think of the adult or adults who live with and take care of you. This might be your dad, mom, stepparents, foster parents, guardians, or adult relatives. *Family* includes these people and sisters, brothers, stepsiblings, or others who share a home with you.

# How to Use This Book

This book has lots of advice and tips you can use on your own. It also includes activities that you and your parents can do together. You can also show it to other adults who help you with your ADHD—like teachers, doctors, counselors, and tutors. Adults who read it with you will learn new ways to help you. And you can work together with them on any special challenges you face.

You can read this book from start to finish—or a little at a time. You might decide to read it for fifteen minutes just before you go to bed. Or you may want to look at certain sections with a parent over the weekend. Because ADHD affects every kid differently, you might not need to read every word. Instead you might concentrate on topics you want to learn more about or need extra help with. Use the book in whatever way works for you and your family.

# You Can Succeed with ADHD

I wrote this book because I care a lot about kids with ADHD. I've met with many of these kids and have worked with them to overcome many challenges. Some common experiences they've shared with me appear in quotes through-out this book. With a little effort, these kids have been able to achieve better grades at school, get along at home, and make (and keep) friends. Each of them learned how to manage ADHD and succeed . . . and *you* can, too!

> Each chapter ends with a fun quiz. (Don't worry—quizzes won't be graded!) You can make photocopies of quizzes and fill them out to see what you've learned.

   I hope this book helps you. I would love to hear how you are using the ideas you read about. You can also write to me if you have any questions or could use help with something. You can send a letter to me at this address:

**Dr. John Taylor**
c/o Free Spirit Publishing
217 Fifth Avenue North, Suite 200
Minneapolis, MN 55401-1299

You can email me at:
help4kids@freespirit.com

# The Six Great Gripes of Kids with ADHD

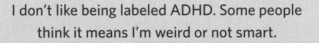

**1.**

I don't like being labeled ADHD. Some people think it means I'm weird or not smart.

**2.**

It's really hard for me to focus at school. Even though I try to do well, I fall behind the other kids.

**3.**

I'm not organized. I lose assignments and forget about the things I'm supposed to do.

**4.**

It's hard for me to control my behavior. I get in trouble with my parents and teachers.

**5.**

I worry about the medicine I have to take for my ADHD. Will it hurt me?

**6.**

Other kids don't understand ADHD. It makes it hard for me to be their friend.

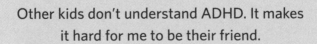

# What Is ADHD?

## What Does ADHD Mean?

**ADHD** stands for **attention deficit hyperactivity disorder.** Kids are given the ADHD label when it's hard for them to stay still, pay attention, and make good decisions. If you've been labeled ADHD, you probably have trouble focusing on your work at school. It might also be hard for you to show good behavior because you want to talk or move around a lot. ADHD affects how you get along with adults and other kids. People might not understand or like what you do or say—even when you don't think anything is wrong.

**FAST FACT:**
About one out of every thirteen kids in the United States is labeled with ADHD.

The good news is that you can take action to manage ADHD. The first step is to understand how it affects you. You probably have some **traits** that create challenges for you. *Traits* are different ways that you think, act, and feel. They affect how you do things and get along with others. If you have been labeled ADHD, you probably have one or more of these four traits:

**Trouble keeping your mouth and body still.** You might find it hard to be still when a parent or teacher wants you to sit quietly. You might move your feet, tap your fingers on a table or desk, talk a lot, or make sounds with your mouth. This trait is called being **hyperactive.** Sometimes people may say that you are *fidgeting* or being *hyper.*

## Kids who are hyperactive say:

"I can't control what my hands and feet do."

"I get yelled at a lot for talking in class."

"I squirm in my chair at school and have to stand up sometimes."

**Trouble staying focused on things that are hard or "boring."** Maybe you have a difficult time taking tests or doing homework. You might have trouble finishing things that you start. Or you may be easily bothered by noises when trying to study. This trait is called being **inattentive.** People might also say that you are *distracted* or that you have a *short attention span*.

## Kids who are inattentive say:

"Any sound in class bothers me—like the lights buzzing or other kids coughing."

"My mind sometimes goes on a road trip."

"It's like I have ten TV channels in my head and I don't know which one to watch."

**Trouble with making decisions too fast.** You might make up your mind quickly without stopping to figure out the best plan. These decisions may end up getting you in trouble. This extra-fast decision-making is called being **impulsive.** Sometimes people may say that you are *careless*.

## Kids who are impulsive say:

"It's like there's an engine inside me that makes me act before I think."

"Sometimes I can't help what I do."

"My mouth says things before I can think of what I *should* say."

**Trouble with making decisions too slowly.** Maybe you take a long time to make decisions because you're afraid of making a mistake. This extra-slow decision-making is called being **indecisive.** People might also say that you are a *perfectionist.*

## Kids who are indecisive say:

"People are always telling me to hurry up and decide."

"It's like my mind gets stuck when I'm trying to figure something out."

"Sometimes I won't make a choice because I can't figure out which one is perfect."

Which of these traits do you have? Here's an activity to help you figure it out.

**1.** Make a photocopy of the list of ADHD traits and behaviors on pages 11–12.

**2.** Use a pencil to check the boxes next to the behaviors that you have a hard time with. Ask your parents to look over the list to see if they agree with the things you've checked.

**3.** Add up the number of checkmarks under each trait and write it in the blank.

**4.** Circle the traits with the most checkmarks. These are your strongest ADHD traits.

# What Are My ADHD Traits?

## Hyperactive?

☐ I talk a lot—even when I'm supposed to be quiet.

☐ I make lots of clicks and sounds with my mouth.

☐ I squirm in my chair and move my hands and feet when I'm sitting.

☐ I run ahead of adults or groups of kids.

☐ I poke, touch, feel, and grab other people or objects.

☐ I say or do things without thinking about them first.

_____ = TOTAL

## Inattentive?

☐ I'm bothered by noises when I'm trying to do schoolwork.

☐ I have trouble paying attention to anything that seems boring to me.

☐ I take longer to finish schoolwork than other students.

☐ I have a hard time concentrating when I take tests.

☐ I daydream or zone out a lot at school.

☐ I forget my teacher's directions.

_____ = TOTAL

continued

# What Are My ADHD Traits? (continued)

## Impulsive?

- ☐ I make people angry because I say or do things without thinking of others.
- ☐ I often forget to plan ahead.
- ☐ I do or say things that are dangerous or hurt others.
- ☐ I get into fights with others.
- ☐ I blurt out in class without raising my hand.
- ☐ I have trouble waiting for my turn.

_____ = TOTAL

## Indecisive?

- ☐ I worry a lot when trying to decide things.
- ☐ I start many new tasks but don't finish them.
- ☐ I take a lot longer to do schoolwork or tests than other kids.
- ☐ I need help from my parents or other adults when making simple decisions.
- ☐ I give up trying to do things because I can't do them perfectly.
- ☐ I get confused when I'm trying to make a decision.

_____ = TOTAL

# The Three Types of ADHD

There are actually three types—or kinds—of ADHD. The labels kids with ADHD get depend on what traits they show at home and school. Here are the different kinds:

**ADHD, Hyperactive-Impulsive type:** Kids with this label are *hyperactive* and *impulsive.* Girls can have this kind of ADHD, but boys are most often given this label.

`JUAN` "I know you're excited to answer, but please remember to raise your hand," said Juan's teacher. "I'm sorry, Ms. Olsen," Juan replied. That was the third time in one day she had to remind him.

Juan understands most things at school, but he thinks things don't go fast enough there. He often blurts out in class or gets out of his chair when he's excited. Juan tries to follow the rules, but it doesn't seem to work. It's like he can't control his body or his mouth. Adults often tell him that he's too hyper and that he needs to slow down. ■

**ADHD, Inattentive type:** Kids with this kind are *inattentive* and *indecisive.* People sometimes call this *ADD.* They leave out the "H" because hyperactivity is not a problem for kids with this kind of ADHD. Of girls who have ADHD, most have this label.

`HEIDI` "Heidi?" The voice of Mr. Donald came to her through a fog. "Yes?" Heidi finally answered. She had been daydreaming about playing with her dog Lucky. "Please pay attention to the lesson," said Mr. Donald. "This kind of math can be hard." "I'm sorry. I'll try," Heidi said.

Heidi has trouble concentrating. No matter how hard she tries to listen, Mr. Donald's lessons sound like "blah, blah, blah." When she is working, even small noises distract her. ■

**ADHD, Combined type:** Kids with this label are *hyperactive* and *inattentive*—or they have some other mix of traits different from the other two kinds of ADHD.

WILL "Please stay in your seat and listen, Will," said Mr. Tanaka. "Sure," Will answered. But a minute later, Will was back over at Rob's desk talking about a great skateboarding trick he'd just learned. "Back to your desk, Will. Right now!" Mr. Tanaka exclaimed.

Almost every day at school is like this for Will. He thinks it's boring. Instead of listening in class, he moves around and talks a lot. Will is easily distracted and gives up on most assignments and tests because he thinks they're too boring or hard. He spends a lot of the school day in the resource room, where Mrs. Adams helps him with his work. ■

If you have been labeled ADHD, you might know about these three different kinds and which one you have. If not, you can look at your answers to the activity on pages 11–12 to figure it out. If your strongest ADHD traits (the ones you circled) are:

**hyperactive and impulsive**

Your label is: ADHD, Hyperactive-Impulsive type (like Juan)

**inattentive and indecisive**

Your label is: ADHD, Inattentive type (like Heidi)

**hyperactive and inattentive**

(or another mix of ADHD traits)

Your label is: ADHD, Combined type (like Will)

It is helpful to know what type of ADHD you have. When you do, you can work on the things that you have the most trouble with.

> You and your dad or mom might want to do the activity on pages 11–12 with a doctor or another one of the professionals talked about in Chapter 3.

# Why Do Some Kids Have ADHD?

That's a good question. Experts believe that kids with ADHD process information differently than most people. These differences in how the brain works can cause kids to show ADHD traits. It's like a bad telephone connection: Different parts of your brain are trying to "talk" to one another, but the line is full of static and the messages can't get through. You might be telling yourself to stay still and pay attention, but part of your brain is missing the message.

People who study ADHD don't know exactly why some people have it. Many think that ADHD is passed on to kids by their parents. Others believe that kids with ADHD have been exposed to certain chemicals.

# What ADHD Does NOT Mean

When you have ADHD, your brain and body are not sick. You don't have bad germs in you. Having ADHD doesn't mean you are stupid, lazy, crazy, bad, or ill. It means that there are some differences in the way your brain works that make you show some ADHD traits.

Having ADHD also means that you have some special skills and talents. Kids with ADHD often have a lot of energy and join in many activities. They're active and often excited to try new things. Many are very creative and have special "smarts."

**Music smarts.** If you're music smart, you might be able to figure out how to play songs really well on a musical instrument. You may also make up your own songs to play and sing.

**Art and color smarts.** Kids who are art and color smart can usually draw, color, and paint very well. They may also have a good eye for color and design.

**Muscle smarts.** Being muscle smart doesn't usually mean being able to lift a lot of weight. It means being good at dancing, running, swimming, sports, and other physical activities.

**Mechanics smarts.** If you're mechanics smart, you might know a lot about how gadgets work. You might enjoy working with wires, wood, bolts, screws, and metal.

**Drama smarts.** Kids who are drama smart are great at acting and remembering lines for plays. They enjoy being on a stage in front of an audience. Some drama smart kids are good at coming up with creative stories or telling funny jokes.

**Computer smarts.** Being computer smart means— duh!—being good at working on computers. Kids who are computer smart often know a lot about the Internet and electronic games.

# CHAPTER 1 QUIZ

No need to worry about grades for this quiz. It's just a fun way for you to show off all you've learned about ADHD in this chapter. You'll find the right answers upside down at the bottom of the page. Good luck!

**1.** Jake has been labeled ADHD. What does ADHD stand for?

　A. **a**wesome, **d**aring, **h**andsome **d**ude

　B. **a**ttention **d**eficit **h**yperactivity **d**isorder

　C. **a**dventurous, **d**reaming, **h**igh-flying, **d**ragon

**2.** Carla has ADHD. Which of these is true about her?

　A. Her body is sick and won't ever get better.

　B. Her brain has germs in it and she can't learn.

　C. Some brain differences make her show ADHD traits.

**3.** Rasheed thinks he might have ADHD. What can he do?

　A. Show this book to a parent and talk about why he thinks he has ADHD.

　B. Hide this book and hope that he starts to calm down without anyone's help.

　C. Give this book away and pretend that ADHD isn't real.

**4.** Sam has ADHD and thinks that reading books is boring. What can Sam learn if he reads *this* book?

　A. How to speak with aliens from a planet named Zatar.

　B. Where to find a stash of buried treasure.

　C. Ways to deal with ADHD at school, at home, and with friends.

**Answers:** 1. B. (Although Jake would also say that he is an awesome, daring, handsome dude!) 2. C. 3. A. 4. C.

# CHAPTER 2

# Make Each Day Go Better

"Sometimes I ask a million questions and bounce around like a rubber ball."

"My teachers say that I'm full of great ideas and they like how excited I am about everything."

"My mom says there's never a dull moment when I'm around!"

It's true that kids with ADHD have some qualities that make them stand out from others. Some of these traits probably make you feel good about yourself. People might be impressed with your high energy and enthusiasm. Or they may encourage your creativity and wild imagination.

The same traits that make you stand out in positive ways also can make you get attention for reasons that aren't so good. Remember that you have many qualities and abilities that you can be proud of. Your ADHD traits probably do create some challenges for you, but you can work on them and succeed. This chapter has three ideas to help you along the way.

How to start? It's all about attitude.

# Think on the Bright Side

Did you know that the way you think about yourself affects how you *feel* about yourself? It's true. Scientists have proven it in experiments. People who think positively are more likely to feel good about themselves.

Kids with ADHD sometimes have a hard time staying positive. They worry that their ADHD traits will cause them to make mistakes. This is a problem because when you think you'll fail or mess up, the chance that you will goes way up.

Let's take a look at some of the negative things that kids with ADHD sometimes think about themselves— and positive thoughts they can have instead.

## If you think:

"My parents and teachers are always mad at what I say or do. It's like they don't think I'm trying to keep my ADHD under control."

"I'll never do well in school. I can't focus on my work or pay attention to what teachers are saying."

## Remember:

You have many unique qualities and a one-of-a-kind personality that you can be proud of. The trick for you is to let your good qualities shine so people can see them. At the same time, you can work on those things about your ADHD that people don't like so much. Keep a positive attitude as you face challenges. You can think:

I'm an important person with lots of potential. My ADHD does make it hard for me to do some things. But I'm learning new ways to pay attention, stay still, and make good decisions. With a positive attitude and practice, I'll keep making progress and succeed.

# Fly Your Decision-Making KITE

You are in charge of you. Nobody else can control your actions. Every moment of your life, *you* are deciding what you will do: how you will act, what you will say, how you will handle a situation. The decision-making KITE is a tool you can use to figure out the very best decision for any situation that might come up.

**K** – Know the situation you face.

**I** – Identify—or figure out— your choices.

**T** – Try the best plan.

**E** – Evaluate your plan (figure out if it worked).

**K** **Know the situation you face.** Figure out as much as you can about a situation. Has it ever happened before? What did you do? Did it work? Who might be able to help you?

**I** **Identify—or figure out—your choices.** Try to come up with a few different ideas to handle a situation. You can call these Plan 1, Plan 2, and Plan 3. Figure out the good things and bad things that might happen with each plan. Will a plan make the situation better? Could it make things worse?

**T** **Try the best plan.** After you've thought about the good and bad parts of each plan, choose the one that you think will work best. Then try your plan.

**E** **Evaluate your plan (figure out if it worked).** Did your plan work? If not, look back at the other plans you came up with. Is there one that might make the situation better? Give that one a try, or—if you're stumped—get the help of an adult.

HAKIM "Can I use the computer now?" Hakim asked. Beth looked up from the screen. "My time's not up yet," she said. Hakim was upset. "But I have to work on my project and this is the only computer in class," Hakim said. "You're hogging it." Beth stayed sitting at the computer. "It's still my turn," she said. "Ask Ms. Williams if you don't believe me."

But Hakim didn't want to ask Ms. Williams. He thought Beth was taking too long. He wanted to use the computer *right now*. Hakim felt himself getting angry—like he might do something bad. Just then he remembered the KITE decision-making tool. He decided to sit down and write out the steps in his notebook. This is what he wrote:

**K** – KNOW THE SITUATION YOU FACE.

I need to use the computer. But Beth says it's still her turn.

**I** – IDENTIFY OR FIGURE OUT YOUR CHOICES.

PLAN 1: Stand beside Beth and ask "Are you done yet?" over and over.

    Good Things: Beth might get tired of me and leave.

    Bad Things: Beth might get annoyed and tell Ms. Williams.

PLAN 2: Forget about my project for now and ask for an extension.

    Good Things: I'll have more time to get my project done on the computer.

    Bad Things: If I can't get an extension, it will be hard for me to finish my project on time.

PLAN 3: Ask Ms. Williams if there's a computer I can use in another part of school.

    Good Things: If Ms. Williams knows about another computer I can use, I can work on my project right away.

    Bad Things: I might have to wait for Beth to finish if there's no other computer available.

**T** – TRY THE BEST PLAN.

Plan 1 could get me in trouble. My project could be late if Plan 2 doesn't work. Plan 3 seems like the best. It can help me to work on my project right now. I'll talk with Ms. Williams about using another computer.

Later, Hakim evaluated his plan:

**E** – EVALUATE YOUR PLAN (FIGURE OUT IF IT WORKED).

Ms. Williams let me go to the media center! There were plenty of computers to work on. I got my project done. And I didn't get in trouble! ∎

# FLY YOUR DECISION-MAKING KITE

## K Know the situation you face.
Write as much as you can about the situation.

_____

_____

## I Identify—or figure out—your choices.
Write down three plans that might make the situation better.
What good things and bad things could happen with each plan?

**Plan 1:** _____

Good Things: _____

Bad Things: _____

**Plan 2:** _____

Good Things: _____

Bad Things: _____

**Plan 3:** _____

Good Things: _____

Bad Things: _____

## T Try the best plan. Which plan do you think will work the best? Why?

_____

## E Evaluate your plan (figure out if it worked).
Did your plan work? If yes, great! Mission accomplished.

If no, go back to the other plans you thought about using. Would one of them work? If yes, try that plan. If not, ask an adult for help.

Whenever you are in situations where you're not sure what to do or are afraid you will make a mistake, you can use the KITE decision-making tool. Don't be afraid to get the help of a trusted adult or friend if you're not sure what decision to make.

## CHECK THIS OUT:

 *The Behavior Survival Guide for Kids* **by Tom McIntyre.** This book has ideas for staying in charge of behavior and making good decisions.

# LEAP Over Your Mistakes

What if you use the KITE decision-making tool and still make a mistake? First, don't feel bad. Everyone makes some mistakes. Your goal should not be to make *no mistakes*—that's impossible. Your goal should be to take advantage of your mistakes by using them wisely. How can you do this? Use them to LEAP over ADHD challenges.

## Remember that mistakes are:

**L** – Learning tools

**E** – Expected

**A** – Accidental

**P** – Proof of effort

Let's take a closer look at how you can LEAP over your mistakes.

**L** **Learning tools.** Mistakes help us to learn. They teach us important lessons. When you make a mistake, you can remember what happened. Then the next time you're in a similar situation, you can change what you do so that things go better.

**E** **Expected.** Mistakes are bound to happen. Why do pencils have erasers? Because mistakes are going to happen. Why is the eraser much bigger than the writing end? Because you're going to make many mistakes. Pencils are like your life. You will try to do many things and make lots of mistakes as you do.

**A** **Accidental.** You can't make a mistake on purpose. Every mistake is an accident. It's okay to have an accident, and it's okay to make a mistake.

**P** **Proof of effort.** Every mistake shows effort. It proves that you were trying to do something. The only way to avoid mistakes is to never try anything. Mistakes also show two other things that start with "P"—**PRACTICE** and **PROGRESS**. With effort, you'll get better at the things you struggle with.

**SHEILA** Sheila has been struggling with spelling tests. A few weeks ago she forgot there was a test. She had to take it without studying. This made Sheila mark the test dates in her assignment notebook. She thought this would solve her spelling test problem. She even made flash cards to study. Unfortunately, Sheila learned another lesson last week—you can't study flashcards if they're lost at the bottom of your locker. Sheila was mad at herself. Her disorganization had caused her to get another bad grade. So she cleaned her locker and began putting all the stuff she had to bring home on one shelf.

The night before this past test, Sheila brought her flash cards home and studied them. Sheila did better on the test. She didn't get 100 percent, but her teacher marked a smiley face on her paper and wrote a note that said, "Nice job, Sheila! You're getting better!" Sheila was happy because she was improving at spelling. ■

Sheila used her mistakes to LEAP over the challenges she had on spelling tests. First, she used each mistake as a **LEARNING TOOL**—each mistake taught her to do something differently. She also remembered that mistakes were **EXPECTED**. No one received 100 percent on every single test. She knew she was trying her best and that her spelling mistakes were **ACCIDENTAL**. Her mistakes were also **PROOF OF EFFORT**. Her teacher's note showed that. It also told her that she was making **PROGRESS**.

# CHAPTER 2 QUIZ

You've learned three ways in this chapter to make each day go better. Now it's time for a quiz. Answers are upside down at the bottom of the page. (Hey, no peeking!)

1. Julio has ADHD and doesn't think anybody likes him. What can he do to keep a positive outlook?

   A. Remember he has qualities that make him likeable.

   B. Believe that the other kids are baloney-brains and don't deserve to be his friend.

   C. Think the only true friends are imaginary ones.

2. Tenisha has a disagreement with a classmate and doesn't know what to do. What is the best advice for Tenisha?

   A. She should ignore the situation and hope it gets better on its own.

   B. She should use the KITE tool to find the best plan.

   C. She should ask her pet cat for advice on what to do.

3. Tom uses the KITE decision-making tool. What does KITE stand for?

   A. **k**eep **i**ce-cream **t**reats **e**asy to find

   B. **k**nowledge **i**s **t**otally **e**xciting

   C. **k**now the situation, **i**dentify your choices, **t**ry the best plan, **e**valuate your plan

4. Sheri tried hard on an assignment but made some mistakes and got a low grade. Which of these is true?

   A. Sheri is lazy and doesn't try hard enough.

   B. Sheri's mistakes are learning tools she can use to LEAP over challenges and do better next time.

   C. Sheri should spend *all* of her time studying.

**Answers:** 1. A. 2. B. 3. C. (Although it's also nice to have ice-cream treats around!) 4. B.

# Getting Help for ADHD

There is some very good news about having ADHD: Many people are available to help you manage it. Parents, teachers, counselors, doctors, and other professionals are some of these people. You can think of them as your ADHD team. These people on your team can help you understand ADHD better and deal with it in the best ways.

This chapter offers the lowdown on how kids are labeled with ADHD. It also has info on professionals you may work with and treatment options you and your family might try.

# Getting Diagnosed with ADHD

Because everyone with ADHD is unique, professionals recommend different treatments for different kids. Some kids take medicine for ADHD, some don't. Some kids work mostly on behavior with professionals, others on paying attention better.

Different professionals can diagnose ADHD—or figure out if you have it. **Psychologists** and **psychiatrists** are some of these professionals. They know a lot about how people think and act. These people can find out whether kids have ADHD by talking with them and giving special tests. The tests may include putting pictures in a certain order, telling a story, or copying designs. Some may be done on a computer. Psychologists and psychiatrists also talk with parents and teachers about how kids act at home and in school. Part of their work is to help kids with ADHD adjust in these places.

**Physicians**—or doctors—understand how our bodies work and help people to stay healthy. Doctors diagnose ADHD by examining kids and talking with them and their families. You might see a **pediatrician,** a doctor who works only with kids. A **neurologist** also might diagnose ADHD. This kind of doctor knows a lot about how the brain works and can tell whether someone has ADHD by measuring how well the **nervous system** is working.

# After You Have Been Diagnosed with ADHD

If you are diagnosed with ADHD, the professionals you worked with will talk with you and your family. They'll help you understand ADHD and show family members ways to help you with it.

There's a good chance you will see a **counselor.** Your counselor could be a psychologist or psychiatrist who diagnosed you with ADHD. It might also be someone a doctor recommends you visit. Counselors have special training for talking with people about their feelings. They listen to what you have to say, and they can help you deal with strong emotions.

Other people you and your family may see are **family counselors** and **social workers.** These people talk with you and your family about ADHD and give advice for making things go better at home. Some families also work with an **ADHD coach**—a person with special training who can help with the challenges that ADHD can create for kids and families.

You probably don't have to see *all* of these people, but most kids see at least one or two professionals after they are diagnosed with ADHD. Whoever you work with, try your best to tell professionals all that you can about your ADHD. Even when it's hard to answer their questions, do your best to give them the scoop on how you're feeling and any challenges you're facing.

You also should ask professionals any questions *you* have. If it's hard for you to remember questions, write them down between visits. When you go to an appointment, you can show your questions to whoever is helping you.

**CHERYL** Cheryl was diagnosed with ADHD last year. Her teacher had noticed that she was very hyper in class. When Mrs. Jones spoke with Cheryl's mom, they agreed she had a lot of energy. Cheryl's mom brought her to see the family doctor. The doctor examined her and suggested Cheryl see a psychologist. Cheryl was nervous, but Dr. Shepherd turned out to be very nice. He gave her some tests on the computer. The tests included putting shapes together and were pretty fun. Cheryl liked that there weren't any right or wrong answers. Dr. Shepherd talked with Cheryl about how she felt. He also talked with Cheryl's mom and teachers.

Dr. Shepherd diagnosed Cheryl with ADHD. He spoke with her and her family about ADHD and ways they could work together to make each day go better. Dr. Shepherd also gave her ideas for getting along better at school.

Today, Cheryl is doing very well. She sees Dr. Shepherd once a month and they talk about how things are going. If Cheryl has any problems at home or school, she will write them down for her visit to Dr. Shepherd. Sometimes she also talks to the guidance counselor at school. She's happy to have so many people to help her out with her ADHD. ∎

Like Cheryl, you can work closely with professionals to figure out the best ways to manage ADHD. The next three sections in this chapter are about medicine. You don't have to read them if you don't take medicine for your ADHD. Instead, you can skip ahead to Chapter 4 on page 41.

# The Lowdown on Medicine

Professionals may decide that you will be most helped by medicine—or "meds." ADHD medicine can help you feel more in control of how you act and what you say. Instead of saying or doing something too fast and getting into trouble for it, you're able to stop, think, and make better decisions. Medicine also can help you pay attention at school and remember things better.

There are many kinds of medicine that can be taken in different ways. Some meds are wafers or liquids you eat or drink. Others are capsules—or pills—that you can swallow with water or take with a meal.

If your doctor wants you to take medicine, you shouldn't feel bad. You can feel good to know that there are meds that might help you. For most kids, one kind of medicine

works the best. Sometimes finding the right one takes a little time. You and the professionals you visit can work together to find one that works for you.

**FAST FACT:**
About three out of four kids with ADHD take medicine for it at some point during treatment.

## What can you do to help? Two things:

**1. Take your medicine.** Take the *exact* amount of medicine your doctor says and follow any other instructions. For example, you might have to take meds at a certain time of day. Or it might be important to eat something when you take it. Even if you're tired or don't feel like taking medicine, it's important that you do. Your doctor won't be able to tell whether it's working if you don't follow instructions exactly.

**2. Tell parents and professionals how the medicine affects you.** Your parents and the other adults who are helping you need to know how well the medicine is working. So it's important to tell them how you feel when you take it. Tell them about the good things that happen—like if you feel calmer and are able to focus better. It's possible that a medicine may have **side effects,** too. These are ways the medicine affects you that don't help you. Side effects usually don't cause any serious health problems, but you should tell a parent right away if you notice them. (There's more information about side effects beginning on page 37.)

# Signs That Tell You Medicine Is Working

If your medicine is working, you'll be able to think more clearly and remember things better. You'll also feel less hyper and more in control of what you say or do. Look for these signs that your medicine is working well:

**You feel calmer.** You don't talk as much— or shout or blurt out as often. You're better at controlling anger and not getting upset. You're more patient and not too eager for everything to happen fast.

"Aaah"

**You can control your body better.** You have more control over your muscles. You can draw better and your writing is neater. You aren't as squirmy and you don't have to move your feet or hands as much. You might have better coordination and be able to play sports or do other physical activities with more skill.

**You can think more clearly and focus better.** It's easier to think about and remember things. You might be able to explain things better to others. It's easier for you to pay attention to your teachers at school.

**You can make better decisions.** You can think more about your actions before you do them. This helps a lot to keep you out of trouble. You'll be able to say "no" to someone who is trying to get you to do something that is bad or wrong.

**You feel nicer.** Others might tell you that you're nicer. You use "please," "thank you," "I'm sorry," and other polite words more often. You share your things more with others. You probably care more about how others feel.

**You feel like helping out.** You might volunteer to help others. It can be easier for you to do chores—without a parent telling you to do them. Maybe you also look for ways to help a teacher at school.

## Side Effects of Medicine

Medicine doesn't always work exactly the way your doctor wants it to. Tell a parent right away if you notice any of these side effects after you start taking medicine:

**You have trouble getting to sleep.** You might feel extra alert and squirmy at night making it hard for you to fall asleep.

**You feel sleepy.** You feel very tired and sleepy in the middle of the day. You might feel as if your brain is in slow motion and all of your thoughts and actions are too slow.

**You get headaches.** If you get headaches when you take the medicine, you might have an allergy to it. Tell your parents right away if you get headaches. They can talk with the doctor and find out what to do.

**You are not hungry.** Medicine can cause changes in your appetite. Sometimes you may need to change the times when you eat. If you don't feel like eating at mealtimes, ask if you can wait until later when you feel hungrier. You also could have a snack of some kind. If there are *major* differences in your appetite, your doctor might want you to try a different medicine.

**Other side effects.** There might be other side effects from the medicine you take. Be sure to talk with your parent and your doctor about *all* of the ways medicine affects you.

■ ■ ■

If you have side effects from medicine, it might not be right for you. Other times a medicine can be right, but you have to take it at another time or in different amounts. Doctors might try these different ways to get rid of side effects:

**1.** Change the kind of medicine you take.

**2.** Change the amount of medicine you take.

**3.** Change the time when you take your medicine.

**4.** Have you take the medicine with certain kinds of food.

Sometimes other actions can help reduce side effects. If you have trouble getting to sleep, you might try taking a shower or bath before bed. Eating a snack with protein in it also can help. You can work with your doctor and parents to find other ways to make sure that medicine helps you without side effects. Medicine won't be right for all kids with ADHD. In these cases, professionals work with kids in other ways to control ADHD traits.

RAUL  Raul was diagnosed with ADHD last year. He had a really hard time concentrating in class and the doctor decided that medicine could help him focus. The medicine did help. Raul was able to pay attention to his teacher and his work. But there was a problem: The medicine sometimes stopped working after Raul came home from school. Raul's dad called the doctor. The doctor said Raul could take a small amount of medicine each day after school. It worked! Raul was able to concentrate better on his homework in the evening. ■

# CHAPTER 3 QUIZ

Now that you know a lot about getting help for your ADHD, you can take this quiz. The correct answers are upside down at the bottom of the page. Have fun!

1. Marty is very hyper at home and school. His parents take him to see a pediatrician. What should Marty do?

    A. Sit on his hands and pretend he isn't hyperactive.

    B. Run around so fast the doctor can't see him (like in cartoons).

    C. Tell the pediatrician about his problems with hyperactivity.

2. Carol talks with a psychologist once a month about her ADHD. What should Carol remember?

    A. Something is wrong with her because she talks to a psychologist.

    B. Many kids with ADHD talk with counselors and psychologists.

    C. Psychologists have x-ray vision.

3. Ahmad takes ADHD meds. What are some of the ways medicine can help him?

    A. ADHD medicine will make him grow wings.

    B. Medicine can help him stay calm and pay attention.

    C. ADHD medicine will make him grow to be 100 feet tall.

4. Juanita started taking ADHD meds two weeks ago. She notices that she isn't mad as often. What should she do?

    A. Tell a parent that she feels calmer since she started taking the medicine.

    B. Forget to tell anyone about what she notices.

    C. Pretend that the medicine turns her into a kangaroo.

**Answers:** 1. C.   2. B.   3. B. (Although it could be cool to fly!)   4. A.

# CHAPTER 4

# Eating the Right Food

It's probably not news to you that having a healthy diet is important. Your parents might tell you a lot to stick with foods that are good for you. If you're often tempted to trade your carrots for a bag of chips, remember this: Healthy foods give your body and brain the fuel they need to stay running in tip-top shape. A good diet not

You and a parent may wish to work with a family doctor or a **nutritionist**—an expert on food—as you read this chapter.

only helps you stay healthy and strong. It also can make it easier for you to stay in charge of ADHD traits. On the flip side, eating some foods can make it extra hard for you to stay still or pay attention.

# Five Nutrients That Can Help You Manage ADHD

Your brain is a hungry part of your body! It wants you to take in not one, not two, not three or four, but *five* kinds of **nutrients**—different parts of food—to keep running smoothly.

**1. Vitamins.** Vitamins help keep your brain cells alive and healthy. When the cells in your brain are in great shape, you're able to stay alert and think clearly. You might think of vitamins as the parts of food that nudge your brain back "awake" when it starts to "drift off." Vitamins also can help improve your mood. When you have the vitamins you need, you feel better about yourself and sad or angry less often. Vitamins also are available as supplements in the form of capsules, liquids, or tablets.

> **Foods and drinks rich in vitamins:** vegetables (including broccoli, lettuce, spinach, carrots, asparagus, and zucchini) • vegetable juices (including carrot, celery, and tomato juice) • fruit (including apples, strawberries, watermelon, and mango) • yogurt • tofu • enriched breakfast cereals

**2. Proteins.** Proteins are super important for kids with ADHD. After your body breaks down the food you eat, the cells in your brain turn the protein into "messengers." Protein messengers carry messages between the different parts of your brain. They let the different parts of your brain "talk" together so you can concentrate and keep your body still.

> **Foods and drinks rich in protein:** milk • cheese • eggs • meat (including beef and chicken) • fish (including salmon, mackerel, and sardines) • nuts (including walnuts, almonds, and pistachios) • seeds (including pumpkin, sunflower, and sesame seeds) • vegetables (including mushrooms, algae, seaweeds, beans, peas, and lentils) • soy • tofu • whole grain oatmeal and puffed wheat • nut butter

**3. Minerals.** Your brain has about 100 billion cells that send messages back and forth to each other all the time. Every time one of those cells sends a message, it uses up some minerals. You can think of minerals as the bursts of energy that different parts of your brain need to communicate with one another. Because your brain is sending messages all the time, it needs a new supply of minerals each day. In addition to eating the right foods, you can also take mineral supplements in capsules or liquids.

> **Foods rich in minerals:** vegetables (including squash, tomatoes, algae, seaweeds, brussels sprouts, and spinach) • nuts (including cashews, Brazil nuts, and pecans) • enriched grains and fruits • meat (including chicken and turkey) • fish (including cod, tuna, and salmon)

**4. Good fats and oils.** You can think of your brain as a big sponge that needs to stay "wet"—or moist—with oils. Good fats and oils help keep the walls of brain cells healthy and flexible. Like vitamins, good fats and oils also help the parts of your brain that are in charge of your mood. Some good fats and oils—like fish oil—are available as supplements.

> **Foods and drinks full of good fats and oils:** raw fruits and vegetables (including cucumbers, tomatoes, and strawberries) • sour cream • milk • eggs • grape seed oil • butter • olive oil • seeds • nuts • fish (including salmon, mackerel, cod, tuna, and sardines)

**5. Water.** Not only is your brain hungry, it's also extremely thirsty! Like good fats and oils, water helps your brain stay moist. Water also keeps your brain at the right temperature and helps it get rid of wastes. It's best if the water you drink has gone through a filter.

> **You should have a glass of water every two hours.** If it's hard for you to drink this much, make sure you give your brain the water it needs in other ways. You can try: vegetable juices (including carrot, celery, and tomato juice) • foods that are juicy (including watermelon, kiwi fruit, citrus fruits, and berries) • mixes of vegetable and fruit juices (like carrot and pineapple)

A healthy diet includes all five of these nutrients. Most food has one or two. That's why it's important to eat many different kinds of food every day. The more nutrients you get, the better your brain and body will work—and the easier it can be to stay in control of ADHD traits.

> **Fresh vegetables and fruit—not the kind that come in a can— have the most nutrients.** The best meats, fruit, vegetables, and milk say "organic" on the package. Organic usually means a food or drink is fresher and has fewer chemicals. While these are best, they also are more expensive. Check with a parent before you buy them.

## SUPERFOODS

Some foods have four or five nutrients. They are called **superfoods.** (Even though they don't wear capes or fight crime!) Some might seem a little strange, but they're healthy options for keeping your body and brain in good shape so you can stay in charge of ADHD traits.

**SALMON, SARDINES, TUNA, COD, AND MACKEREL** that lived in the ocean are loaded with protein, minerals, and healthy fats.

**SUPERFOOD GRAINS AND NUTS** include walnuts, pistachio nuts, Brazil nuts, cashews, pumpkin seeds, sunflower seeds, oats, wheat, and sesame seeds.

**MILK** is a superfood—well, okay, a "superdrink." Whole milk is usually best for kids with ADHD. If you are allergic to cow's milk, you can try goat's milk, soymilk, nut milk, or rice milk.

**EGGS** are superfoods with tons of protein and minerals.

**SUPERFOOD VEGETABLES** include spinach, asparagus, kale, celery, zucchini, watercress, broccoli, cauliflower, sprouts, lentils, cucumber, cabbage, carrots, bamboo shoots, bok choy, Chinese pea pods, okra, squash, algae, seaweeds, water chestnuts, tomato, leeks, lettuce (not iceberg), onions, beets, brussels sprouts, jicama, yams, peas, beans, sweet potatoes, and soy.

What do bee pollen, royal jelly, wheat grass, and freshwater bluegreen algae have in common? (No, the answer is not that they're part of a sorcerer's potion.) They're super supplements that can help you get the nutrients you need. Some supplements are available at supermarkets. A parent might want to look for others online or at health food stores. Bee pollen and royal jelly are rich in many vitamins, minerals, and healthy fats. Wheat grass is rich in Vitamin C, minerals, and other important nutrients. Freshwater bluegreen algae has many nutrients in it.

# Four Foods to Watch For

Scientists have found that some foods and drinks can make ADHD traits worse. These foods and drinks can make it hard for kids' brains to work well. Like all of the ideas in this chapter, it's a good idea for your parents to talk with a doctor or nutritionist about food options that are best for you.

**1. Foods and drinks you're allergic to.** You may be allergic to some foods and drinks. Common food allergies for kids are wheat, skim milk, oranges, corn, yeast, nuts, pork, chocolate, eggs, peanuts, and soy.
Even though many of these foods
have nutrients you need, they can
make your ADHD worse if you
are allergic to them. Tell parents
right away if you get a skin rash,
a headache, an upset stomach, or
rosy red cheeks or ears soon after
eating or drinking something.

**2. Foods with bad fats and oils.** Some fats and oils can help your brain stay in top form. Others can make it harder for your brain to work well. Bad fats and oils are often found in food that is "processed"—made in factories. Margarine and shortening are two examples of processed food. Most cooking oils—like vegetable, corn, peanut, and cottonseed oil—also can be bad for ADHD. (Olive oil is a better option for you.) French fries and potato and corn chips usually are fried in these oils and are not good food choices for kids with ADHD.

**3. Foods high in carbohydrates.** Carbohydrates include sugars often found in breads, cereals, and pasta. Your body does need carbohydrates. But foods high in carbs often have few of the vitamins, minerals, good fats, or protein you need. Some common foods that are high in carbohydrates include rolls, bread, pancakes, waffles, rice, macaroni, and spaghetti.

Eating these foods in moderation is okay. (Whole wheat breads, cereals, and pastas are best.) Just be sure you're also eating foods with enough protein, vitamins, minerals, and other nutrients at the same time.

**4. Foods and drinks with harsh chemicals.** Some harsh chemicals can react badly with kids who have ADHD. Often dyes (which turn food bright colors) and **preservatives** (which help keep food fresh) cause ADHD traits to get worse. The artificial flavors and sweeteners often found in soda, desserts, sports drinks, and candy also can be bad for you.

If you do want to have some sweets (and who doesn't?), it's better for you to have those with real sugar. Real honey, brown sugar, maple syrup (from the tree), molasses, stevia, and fructose are all better than artificial flavors or sweeteners.

# Helping Plan Your Menu

Now that you know what foods can be good—and bad—for you, you can help to plan your own menu. Sit down with a parent and think of the foods you like. Look through this chapter together and write down some ADHD-friendly foods that sound good to you.

You can plan for breakfast, lunch, dinner, and snacks for after school and bedtime. To get you started on your list, let's look at some healthy options.

**Main dishes.** Nutritious main dishes have foods that are rich in the vitamins, minerals, protein, and good oils and fats. These dishes may include fish, chicken, eggs, beef, vegetables, turkey, and cheese. Which ones sound good to you?

### Magnificent Main Dishes

sweet potato-carrot casserole • mixed vegetable casserole with cheese • chicken-noodle casserole • baked or broiled chicken or turkey • spaghetti with turkey or meat balls • macaroni and cheese • meat loaf • omelet • vegetable soup • taco or burrito stuffed with meat or veggies • stir-fried chicken or tofu sticks • stuffed green peppers • tortilla and black bean casserole • cheeseburger patty • tabouli • homemade pizza with veggies on it • baked stuffed squash • grilled cheese sandwich • linguini with pesto sauce • broiled or baked salmon • spinach and cheese casserole • lasagna

**Side dishes.** Side dishes usually are smaller than main dishes. They can complement main dishes. That means if you have a main dish with lots of minerals and protein, you'll probably want to choose side dishes that have vitamins and good fats and oils. Some super-good side dishes include vegetables like sweet potatoes, broccoli, spinach, cauliflower, beans, peas, cheese, and mushrooms. How do these sound?

**Splendid Side Dishes**

bean casserole • lentils with barley • split peas with bulgur • black beans with rice • peas or green beans steamed and buttered • tofu fritters • lentil or bean loaf • refried beans • Chinese vegetables • minestrone soup • miso soup • Japanese soba noodles • grilled or broiled veggies • steamed carrots or zucchini • sautéed spinach or veggies • veggies with maple syrup or cream cheese • raw veggies with dips • mixed peas and carrots • stuffed tomato • veggies with cheese sauce • sweet potato fries • veggie soups

**Salads.** A salad can be a great addition to a meal—or a meal in and of itself! Salads are very good for kids with ADHD. You might like yours with lettuce, cabbage, celery, carrots, green peppers, onions, or other vegetables. You can get more protein by adding in some beans, boiled egg, chicken, nuts, or cheese. You might also give fruit salad a try—add bananas, pears, pineapple, melon, apples, or other fruit favorites. When you have fruit salad, make sure also to eat a food that has protein.

**Snacks.** Snacks are important. They keep your brain (and stomach) satisfied between meals. It's a good idea to have a snack after school and at bedtime. For those times you're on the go, carry snacks with you in a sandwich bag or in your pocket. The best snacks for kids with ADHD have protein in them.

**Super Snacks**

baby carrots and celery with a nut butter • raw veggies with cream cheese or bean dip • rice cakes with cream cheese • black bean or pinta chips • a bluegreen algae snack bar • turkey or salmon patty • egg salad • fresh fruit (pears, papaya, pineapple, melons, lemons, dates, figs, avocado, guava, breadfruit, coconut, kiwi, pomegranate, and bananas) • nuts • string cheese • pumpkin seeds • sunflower seeds • pretzels • bits of frozen veggies • homemade trail mix • popcorn • dried bananas • peanut butter on crackers

You don't have to try or follow all of these suggestions. You might want to mix things up—have a main dish for a side dish, or vice versa. Some meals you and your family will want to have salads or soups with—others not. You might have a special snack not listed here. By all means, enjoy! Just make sure you're getting a good balance of nutrients—and avoiding foods that make your ADHD traits worse. To help you do this, work with a parent to create a weekly menu.

Because you're not at home all of the time, you won't always have a choice about what there is for you to eat. At school, for example, you might have to choose from the dishes that are available for all students. If it's hard for you to make good food choices there, you may work with a parent to prepare lunches to bring to school. You also can think about carrying ADHD-friendly snacks when you're playing outside, visiting people, or doing other activities away from home.

# Grocery Shopping and Preparing Your Food

Many kids with ADHD like to help their parents do the shopping. After you make a list of all of your food ideas, you and a parent can use it to buy groceries. You can help pick out good fruits and vegetables, add up costs on a calculator, or take part of the shopping list with your own cart. You also can help a parent decide which foods to get by reading the labels. Together you can find the foods that have protein, minerals, good fats, and vitamins in them. You don't have to stop at shopping for groceries. You also can help prepare your food at home.

# CHAPTER 4 QUIZ

Okay, so now you have the dish on foods that can help you stay in charge of ADHD traits. Are you feeling up to taking on this quiz? All right then, dive in! You can check your answers at the bottom of the page.

**1.** What are five nutrients that are good for you?

   A. vitamins, proteins, minerals, good fats and oils, water

   B. ants, millipedes, spiders, good gnats and earthworms, pond scum

   C. bat wings, snake tongues, mice tails, good gremlins and gargoyles, ectoplasm

**2.** How do proteins help kids with ADHD?

   A. Proteins turn on "smart" genes in kids so they become geniuses.

   B. Proteins help carry messages between different parts of your brain.

   C. Proteins can help kids become invisible in sticky situations with parents.

**3.** Superfoods can be good for kids with ADHD. What are superfoods?

   A. Crime-fighting vegetables in tights and capes.

   B. Foods high in many different kinds of nutrients.

   C. Foods made up of radioactive energy from the earth's core.

**4.** What is the best snack for kids with ADHD?

   A. a chocolate-covered tarantula topped off with whipped cream

   B. protein-alicious pumpkin and sunflower seeds

   C. a slice of red ant and mosquito pie

**Answers:** 1. A.   2. B. (Although turning invisible would be pretty cool, too!)   3. B.   4. B.

# Life on the Home front

"Sometimes my dad gets mad at stuff I do, but he knows I'm trying my best."

"When I'm hyper, my big sis tells me to chill."

"Even though I try to behave, my grandma is usually angry with me for something."

Because you spend so much time with family members, they're in a great position to give you ideas and support as you work to succeed with ADHD. Of course, not everything in family life is perfect. Kids with ADHD—like *all* kids—sometimes find it hard to get along with parents and siblings. Conflicts can come up. Parents might get angry at things you do. Brothers and sisters may annoy you. Also, some routines—like waking up, doing chores, and going to bed—can

be especially challenging for kids with ADHD.

Some challenges *will* come up at home. This chapter has many ideas for working with your family to overcome them. The professionals you work with will have other ideas for you and your family.

> **Remember:** When you read about *parents* in this book, think of the adult or adults who live with and take care of you. This might be your dad, mom, stepparents, foster parents, guardians, or adult relatives. *Family* includes these people and sisters, brothers, stepsiblings, or others who share a home with you.

# Connect with Parents and family Adults

Even though adults at home might be your biggest supporters, they also might seem like the biggest nags or party poopers on the planet. You probably don't get to do *all* of the things you want to do. (You might be the first kid in the history of the world if you did!) Maybe a parent gets upset about your mistakes—even when you're trying to follow rules and make good decisions.

## CHECK THIS OUT:

 **It's My Life—Family (www.pbskids.org/itsmy life/family).** Visit this Web site for fun info on family life. It has games, videos, and advice from other kids on how to get along at home.

The good news is you can work with family adults on challenges. Along the way you can make them happy by showing them you are doing your best. How?

**Mind your manners, please!** Parents (and other family members) like kids to be polite. You can use words like "please," "thank you," and "excuse me." When you make mistakes, you can apologize. If there's something you can do to make up for a mistake, do it. For example, you can wipe up water if you spill or return something that you may have taken. When you apologize, you also can say that you will do your best not to make that mistake again. Then you can use the LEAP tool on page 26 to help make sure you don't.

| Rude Words: | Smooth Words: |
| --- | --- |
| *"I want that toy."* | *"May I please have that toy?"* |
| *"I'm going for a bike ride."* | *"May I please go for a bike ride?"* |
| *"Get outta my way!"* | *"Excuse me. May I get through?"* |
| *"Gimme some milk right now!"* | *"Could you please pour me a glass of milk?"* |
| *"It's not my fault. I didn't try to hit the window."* | *"I'm sorry I broke the window."* |

**Join in family activities.** If a parent wants the family to sit together for a meal or talk, join in. Even if you're playing a game or doing something fun, try to join your family quickly so that they won't have to wait for you. It's important to show the adults who care for you that you want to be part of the family. Even if the activity seems boring—like doing the dishes together or getting in the car to go somewhere—try to join in quickly.

**Expect each family member to be treated differently.** Are you the exact same as your brother or sister? Of course not! You have your own unique qualities and traits. You also probably have your own rules in family life. That's why it's important not to get upset if siblings get to do things that you don't. When family adults set rules, they are thinking about what is best for you. Try not to say things like, "But he gets to stay up until ten," or "Why does she get to watch that TV show?" They have rules they believe are important for you—not anyone else. If you think a parent is truly being unfair about something, use polite words to make your case. For example, you could start with, "May I talk with you about the shows I get to watch?"

**Find ways to help out.** Parents love it when kids offer to help with chores or do little favors for others. If you notice that the kitchen counter is full of crumbs, grab a dishcloth and clean it off. If there's mud on the floor, get out the broom and get your "sweep" on. You'll be amazed at how happy your mom or dad will be when you help out in extra ways.

**Take time outs.** If you're talking with a parent about something that is making you angry, take a time out.

You can say something like, "I'm getting upset, Mom. Can I go to my room to think about this for a minute? When I come back can we talk about it again?" This is a great way to avoid blowing up, arguing, and making a situation worse.

> # QUICK TIP:
> When you take a time out, think about ways to make a situation better. You might use the KITE decision-making tool on page 22.

**Show that you care.** Everyone likes to be treated with kindness. Family adults are no exception. How can you show you care? You could make your parents a card telling them how much you love them. Or do something as simple as giving them compliments about things they do. For example, you might say, "Great dinner, Dad." When you show kindness, adults at home remember it.

# Get Along with Brothers and Sisters

Some things you do to connect with parents also can help you get along better with brothers and sisters. For example, being polite is a great way to get along with *anyone*. But you probably already know that it can take more than being polite to make things go smoothly with siblings, stepsiblings, or other kids you live with. You can try these ways to be a super "sib":

**Respect siblings' things.** One thing that can *really* bother siblings is taking their things without asking. To you, it might seem like no big deal to borrow a CD from your brother, but it might be a big deal to him. If you want to use or borrow something that isn't yours, it's important to ask first.

**Respect siblings' privacy.** If a sibling has his or her own room, stay out! If you share a room, don't dig through a sib's stuff. Why? All people have special areas that are important to them. When you don't respect the privacy of brothers or sisters, they can get very upset. Respecting others' privacy includes letting them talk on the phone without listening in. It's also impolite to hover around the computer while a sibling is working on something or surfing the Web.

**Respect siblings' time.** When you're really wrapped up in something, it can be a real drag to have to stop. This might happen if you're playing a game and a sibling wants to quit. When someone wants to stop playing, agree to stop. You might find a fun game or activity you can do on your own.

**Be aware of siblings' friends.** Pay special attention to times when your sibs have friends around them. When brothers and sisters are with others, they might not act in the same ways they do at home when no friends are around. Siblings are often easily embarrassed. Try extra hard to "put your best foot forward" when siblings' friends are around. If you're not sure how, talk with a parent.

**Play win-win games.** Have you ever noticed that people can get pretty intense when they're trying to win a game? If arguments break out when you play games with siblings, there's something you can do: Change the rules of games so that everyone playing wins. One fun win-win game is to play catch while counting the number of times you can throw a ball back and forth before someone drops it. Indoors you might take turns hitting a balloon upward so it doesn't touch the floor.

**Do kind things.** What can you do to be kind? You might volunteer to do a chore for a sibling. You also can give compliments. At a birthday or holiday, give cool gifts that will make siblings happy. These gifts don't have to cost a lot of money. You could work with a parent to bake your sib's favorite cookies. Thank-you notes—like "Thank you for helping me with my homework"—are nice. So are coupons—like one that says "Good for one game of Crazy Eights."

**Use the "I want to get along with you" tool.** What if a sibling is doing something that is bothering you? Instead of flipping your lid, try using a three-part message that can help you get along with a brother or sister. Say the three parts in this order:

**1.** "Please stop _____"
   (then say what your brother
   or sister is doing).

**2.** "Please do _____"
   (then say what you'd like a
   sibling to do instead).

**3.** "If you do that, I'll _____"
   (then say a favor you will do).

   For example, if your sister keeps talking to you while you are trying to read, you could say:

**1.** "Please stop talking to me while I'm reading my homework."

**2.** "Please go to the other room and wait for me. Maybe you can color a picture."

**3.** "If you do that, I'll play checkers with you as soon as I'm done reading."

# Tough Stuff in Families

Some routines and situations can be especially hard for kids with ADHD. You can try these tips for dealing with things you might struggle with at home.

## GETTING READY IN THE MORNING

Some kids with ADHD have trouble waking up in the morning. Parents can get worried or upset if it takes you a long time to get going. Often there isn't much time to get ready, and conflicts can come up that upset everyone. If this sounds familiar, try these ideas for making mornings go better.

**Use a loud alarm clock.** An alarm clock isn't any help if you can't *hear* it. Make sure yours is turned up loud enough to wake you up. Another tip: Place the alarm clock far from your bed so you have to get up to shut it off. That way you won't be tempted to roll over, hit snooze, and go right back to sleep.

**Ask for water.** Having a drink of water can help you get going in the morning. You might also ask your mom or dad to wipe your forehead and cheeks with a damp cloth to help you wake up.

**Use a timer.** Use a timer that tells you how long you have before you must leave for school. Set it right when you get up and watch it to be sure you're on track to leave on time.

**Set your clothes out at night.** Decide the night before what you'll wear in the morning. Then put your clothes in a spot where you can find them easily. This way, you won't have to hunt all over the place for a stray sock or T-shirt. Keeping your schoolbag near your bedroom door also is a good idea.

## STAYING ORGANIZED

Many kids with ADHD are very disorganized. Their rooms often are messy and they sometimes have trouble finding the important things they need. Why does organization matter? Well, losing your backpack under a heap of dirty clothes is a sure way to make yourself late for school. Keeping your room (and other rooms that you use) neat can help routines go better. If you share a room, you and your sibling can work together to make sure everything is organized and clean.

**Use shelves and baskets.** Putting your things in cupboards, drawers, or huge boxes can make them hard to find. An easy way to keep track of your things is to put them on shelves. When you use shelves, you can *see* everything and find what you need without

## QUICK TIP:

If you have a lot of smaller things that go together, you might use baskets. Baskets are great for storing puzzles, game pieces, or other toys with small parts. Put the baskets on your shelves and label them.

looking in a hundred different places. Many kids with ADHD have shelves close to the floor and higher on the wall. Shelves also can be added to closets.

**Use a hamper or laundry basket.** Your room should have a place where you can put dirty clothes. Use a basket or hamper so dirty laundry doesn't get mixed in with your clean clothes—or piled up on your floor or bed.

**Keep things neat and clean.** What's one sure way to lose your things? Forget to clean your room. For example, if you don't make your bed, you won't know if you've accidentally left something that you need under the covers. Or if you let stacks of junk pile up, you won't be able to find the things you really need. Use a wastebasket for trash. You can empty the basket once a week.

> ## QUICK TIP:
> Find one place for every single thing that you need. When you're done using something, return it to its place.

Also, many kids with ADHD are allergic to dust. Dust—and other **allergens**—can make ADHD traits get worse. That's why it's important to sweep or vacuum your floor once a week, including under beds, desks, and chairs. Don't forget to wipe the dust from desktops and shelves.

## MAKING CHORES GO BETTER

Family life goes best when everyone is involved—in the fun stuff and in the work. There might be ways a parent asks you to pitch in at home. Even if chores seem like a bore, it's important to do your part. When you do, you show that you appreciate your family and home. How can you make chores go better?

**Make a "chores chart."** Working together, your family can create a chores chart. Put the chores across the top of the chart and the days of the week down the side. Then fill in the chart with the name of who will do that chore on that day.

| CHORES CHART | VACUUM | WALK DOG | WASH DISHES |
|---|---|---|---|
| MONDAY | | | |
| TUESDAY | | | |
| WEDNESDAY | | | |

**Ask for some choice.** Ask your parent to let you *choose* one or two chores to do each day. If there are many chores to be done, do certain duties on some days and other duties on different days. If you do this, you can have two chores charts—one for Mondays, Wednesdays, and Fridays, and one for the other days.

> **QUICK TIP:**
> Every few days (or weeks), your family can change who does what chores. Be sure to update your chores chart.

## GETTING TO SLEEP

Some kids with ADHD have a hard time calming down at the end of the day and falling asleep. This can cause problems with parents who want to be sure kids get the rest they need. What can you do if you're not tired at the end of the day?

**Take a bath or shower.** Enjoy a long bath or shower before going to bed. Having a soak can help you calm down and feel ready to sleep.

**Have something to look at.** It might be easier for you to get to sleep if you have something to watch in your room. You could use a nightlight or a lamp with slowly moving colors. You also could try watching an aquarium with fish in it or a computer screen saver.

**Find something calm to do.** Some kids with ADHD wind down by reading or doing word puzzles in bed. Others like to listen to stories or music on a CD. Some CDs have relaxing sounds of ocean waves or running water.

**Relax your muscles.** Try tightening your muscles, then relaxing them, over and over while listening to a relaxing tape or CD.

**QUICK TIP:**
Page 101 has directions for a muscle relaxation exercise.

**Sleep in a cool room.** Most kids with ADHD fall asleep easier if they are in a cool room and under a thick blanket. In the summer, a fan can help keep your room cool.

**Have a snack.** If you're hungry, it can be hard to sleep. Eating a nutritious snack (especially one with protein) can help you feel sleepy.

# Have fun Together

There's one last thing you can do with your family to make life at home great: Have fun together! Sharing fun experiences is one of the best ways to keep family life going smoothly. There are all kinds of ways to have fun together.

What fun activities does your family enjoy? Take advantage of these times to build strong relationships. Are there other fun things you think your family should do? Try making a "Fun Idea List" with your parents. Keep this list in a place where all family members can find it. This way you'll always have plenty of ideas for doing cool things together. And you also can do some on your own if you feel bored at home.

Not sure where to start with your "Fun Idea List"? Page 68 has a long list of ideas for having fun with family (and on your own).

### Outdoor Activities

go camping • go fishing • hike or walk together • go swimming • bike together • go jogging • play kickball, softball, or another game • have a water fight (or play in a sprinkler) • go ice skating • go sledding • play hopscotch • play freeze tag • shoot baskets or play "21" • play Frisbee • play badminton • go inline skating • skateboard • wash the car • mow the lawn • play baseball • write on a sidewalk with chalk • make a popcorn or fruit-drink stand • have a water balloon toss • look at stars and the moon through a telescope • work in a garden • throw around a football • play wall ball • jump rope

### Indoor Activities

go bowling • play cards • play table games like checkers, chess, dominoes, or Chinese checkers • use a tape recorder to do a pretend radio or TV interview • do gymnastics • play trivia or board games • read together • build something (for example, a bird feeder) • train, play with, or groom a pet • listen to music • use a chemistry or electronics kit • bake something • write or email a friend • surf the Web • draw, color, or paint • complete crossword or hidden word puzzles (or make your own) • dance • work on a puzzle • make a collage • sing or play a musical instrument • work on a collection • make art with clay • learn to juggle • view and sort family photos • learn magic tricks • put together a model • make holiday decorations • play computer games • dress up in old clothes

# CHAPTER 5 QUIZ

You can use the ideas in this chapter to help make family life more enjoyable for everyone. Here's a quiz you can take to test how much you've learned. You'll find the correct answers upside down at the bottom of the page.

**1.** Which of these ways will help you get along with a parent or another family adult?

A. Reorganize the living room furniture without asking.

B. Mow the lawn in strips that spell out your name.

C. Use polite words and offer to help around home.

**2.** Keiko's little brother is bothering her while she tries to do homework. What should she do?

A. Switch siblings with a friend.

B. Use the "I want to get along with you" tool.

C. Tell her brother to fly to Jupiter.

**3.** Getting ready on time in the morning is a challenge for Brad. What should he do?

A. Make it his goal to sleep until noon every day of the year.

B. Use a loud alarm and set a timer that shows how much time he has before he must leave the apartment.

C. Pretend he doesn't know when school starts. (Maybe he won't have to go!)

**4.** Sasha is tired of washing dishes and cleaning the bathroom. What could she do?

A. Go on strike.

B. Complain and complain and complain.

C. Ask her mom if she can change the chores she's responsible for.

**Answers:** 1. C. 2. B. 3. B. (Although a break from school would be nice!) 4. C.

# Six Ways to Succeed at School

"It's hard for me to keep up with the rest of the kids in my class."

"I have a tough time with English, but I'm really good at math."

"My handwriting is so messy that even I can't read it."

Many kids with ADHD enjoy being at school. But most have challenges there, too. It's often hard for ADHD kids to pay attention to teachers. Kids who are hyperactive often struggle to sit still or stay quiet. If they move or talk a lot, teachers may get upset at them for disrupting class.

You might have these or different challenges. This chapter has six ideas that can help you at school. You can run some of them by your teachers and guidance counselor. They might have other ideas to help you succeed.

# 1. A Great IDEA at School

Many kids with ADHD are involved in **special education** at school. Special ed is for kids who have LD (learning differences). Some people who don't understand LD might say it means someone is not smart. That's not true. Kids with LD can be as smart as anyone—they just learn in different ways. In the United States, a law called **IDEA (Individuals with Disabilities Education Act)** makes sure that schools teach kids with LD in the ways they learn best. Some other countries have similar laws.

When kids have LD, they take tests that show what parts of school they need help with. Teachers, counselors, and other adults at school look at these tests. Then they meet together with parents to create an **IEP (Individualized Education Plan).** An IEP is exactly what it sounds like—it's a *plan*. It explains ways that you learn best at school.

If you are in special education, you might go to a **resource room** (or **resource class**) for at least part of the day. It's here that **resource teachers** can help with subjects you have a hard time with. Resource teachers have special training to help students study and learn in the best ways. Some kids with ADHD also go to rooms for students who have **behavior disorders**—or **BD.** In these classrooms, kids who have trouble showing good behavior in school get help from a teacher with special training.

## CHECK THESE OUT:

 **LD Online Kidzone (www.ldonline.org/kidzone).** This fun site for kids with LD has games, tips, quizzes, and info that can help you do well in school. You also can look at writing and art from kids just like you—or submit your own creative work.

 *The Survival Guide for Kids with LD* **by Gary Fisher and Rhoda Cummings.** This book has lots of ideas you can use to succeed with LD in school, at home, and with friends.

# 2. Work with Teachers and Counselors

Teachers and counselors are part of your ADHD team. They want to help you succeed with ADHD. What can you do to help? First, giving a strong effort is important. Adults at school are giving you all of the help they can. You can do your part by trying hard.

Even when you're doing your best, tough spots can come up at school. It can seem as if teachers don't understand how hard it is for you to do some things. Maybe you think they notice only your mistakes. When you're frustrated, you might start to do or say something that can get you in trouble. **STOP**! Take a time out. You might say to a teacher, "Can we talk about this later? I want to think about it for a while."

> When you are taking a time out, you can use the KITE decision-making tool (see page 22) to figure out a way to make the situation better.

Kids with ADHD often go to a resource room when they're upset or need help. Many also regularly visit the guidance office. Guidance counselors work with kids to handle strong emotions they have at school. They can help you solve any problems that come up with teachers or other kids.

**MOHAMMED** "For the last time, Mohammed, please be quiet." It was Mr. Cantrell. Mohammed looked up. He'd been answering a classmate's question. "But I was just helping Cari," Mohammed started to explain. Mr. Cantrell cut him off. "Do you know what quiet study time means?" Mohammed felt himself getting very mad. He had been trying to do a good thing by helping Cari. Now Mr. Cantrell was talking to him in a mean way and Mohammed felt like he was going to explode. He felt like calling the teacher names and throwing things. That's when Mohammed remembered time outs. "Can we talk about this later, Mr. Cantrell?" Mr. Cantrell just shook his head and sat at his desk. It took a lot of effort, but Mohammed stayed quiet and calm the rest of class. He used the KITE decision-making tool and decided to try making the situation better by talking to the resource teacher, Mrs. Langer.

After class he went to see Mrs. Langer. He told her that the way Mr. Cantrell talked to him made him angry. The resource teacher listened to his story. "You'll still have to be quiet in class," Mrs. Langer said. "But you handled this very well. I'll talk with Mr. Cantrell about how he talks to you." Mohammed was happy. He was getting help with his problem—and he didn't even get in trouble! ∎

## CHECK THIS OUT:

 **It's My Life—School (www.pbskids.org/itsmy life/school).** Make this stop on the Web for the lowdown on everything from test stress to time management. Also find ideas for getting along with teachers and solving homework hassles.

# 3. Move in A-Okay Ways

Many kids with ADHD have a hard time staying still and quiet during class. If this is true for you, you probably know it makes teachers angry because you're not paying attention—and you're making it hard for others to listen. If you take medicine for your ADHD, it probably helps you stay calm in class. You also might have an IEP that has ideas for times when you feel very hyper in class. Here are some other things you can do when you feel squirmy. Make sure they're okay with your teacher before you try them.

**Move in ways that no one notices.** If you feel hyper, try to move in ways that no one notices. You might lean your body very slowly a little in one direction, then the other. You could twirl your thumbs under your desk, tap your leg, or press your hands together. You might also try moving your toes but not your feet—make your toes aim up and down in your shoes. Stretching quietly sometimes also can help.

> **QUICK TIP:**
> Your teacher also may let you rub a soft cloth, hold a piece of yarn, or squeeze a soft ball at your desk.

### Volunteer to help your teacher.

You might run an errand for your teacher. Ask if you can be the person to take notes or books to other adults in the school. You might also help hand out papers or take part in a class demonstration.

**Move around in the classroom.** Some teachers let students with ADHD use two desks, one on each side of the room. If there are no extra desks, you might go sit at the back of the room or in a play area when you feel an urge to move. If you are able to sit in different areas, move slowly and quietly. Bring your assignment or book along so you can continue working.

**Take a break.** Some kids with ADHD have permission to leave the classroom when they feel hyper. Most often these kids will go to the resource room to settle down. Some kids with ADHD have "quiet signals" for teachers when they need to leave class. For example, they might hold up a colored card. Teachers will then nod "yes" or shake their heads "no" to tell kids whether they can leave.

**Burn off energy outside of class.** Try to use lunch, recess, and gym as times to move around. Extracurricular activities also are a great way to use up energy. You might try sports like soccer, basketball, volleyball, or gymnastics. You could also try out for the school play or marching band.

# 4. Focus on the Right Things

Kids with ADHD often have trouble paying attention at school. Many are distracted by noises in the classroom. Others zone out during lessons or find it hard to concentrate on work. Kids who have trouble paying attention often are helped by medicine. These ideas also can help you concentrate in class. You'll want to work with a teacher to find the best ways for you to stay focused.

**Find the right seat.** Usually the best place for your desk is near the front of the room in the row farthest from the hall. It also helps if you don't have kids sitting on both sides of you. Your desk should face away from the door and you should be able to see the teacher well.

Kids with ADHD are often bothered by bright light. To help this, you might ask for a seat far from windows. If your classroom has groups of desks, the best group for you is near a wall away from the door.

**Stay involved in discussions.** Look at your teacher and listen closely to lessons. Raise your hand and make comments. If you don't understand something and start to daydream, raise your hand and ask about it.

**Stop sounds from distracting you.** Kids with ADHD can be easily distracted by noises—even small ones. A teacher might let you wear earphones or earplugs when you are working on assignments. There might be a quiet part of the classroom where you can concentrate better. Some teachers play soft music or turn on a fan or air filter to help students focus. These steady sounds can block out distracting noises.

**Keep your desk clear.** Keep your desk clear except for the assignment you're working on. Doing one thing at a time can help you stay focused. Some kids find that it also helps to do work on a clipboard. You might attach a pen or pencil to the clipboard with a string.

**Break up tasks into small chunks.** Breaking up assignments is a great way to stay on track. How does this work? Say there are twenty math problems on a sheet. Your teacher might ask you to check in after you have done the first ten. After you've checked in, your teacher will ask you to do the rest of the problems.

# 5. Stay Organized

School is *much* easier when you can find everything you need. Unfortunately, kids with ADHD often have big problems when it comes to organization. It can be very frustrating when you don't get credit for an assignment because you lose it or forget to hand it in. If your desk is a mess and your backpack is a black hole, try these tips to stay on top of your work.

**Use a three-ring binder.** A three-ring binder is a great tool for staying organized. It works as one place where you can find everything you need for school. Follow these steps to create a prize-winning binder:

1. Include an assignment notebook or homework chart inside your binder so it's the first thing you see.

2. Add a small zipper pouch to your binder. Inside it, put pencils, pens, erasers, a calculator, a small ruler, tissues, highlighters, and anything else you need at school.

3. Add colored dividers to separate the subjects you have at school.

4. Add a notebook or loose paper to the binder for each subject.

5. Store all "to do" homework in the pocket of the inside front cover of your binder.

6. Include a pocket folder in your binder that is only for *finished* homework. Put all homework in this folder when you're done.

> **IMPORTANT:**
> Once each week go through your binder and pull out the old papers. Check with your teacher to make sure you don't need them anymore, then recycle them.

**Clean your desk and locker.** Keep your desk and locker neat so you can always find what you need. Once each week, remove everything that doesn't belong. Check with your teacher if you're not sure you can recycle or throw something away. If you have anything that belongs to someone else, return it.

**Look at your assignment notebook or homework planner.** It's the end of a long day, and you're glad it's time to go home. What's one last thing you should do before you leave? Look over your assignment notebook or homework planner. Make sure you have all the materials you'll need to study and do your homework that night.

Your books won't do you a lot of good if they're stuck in your locker all night!

AHA, EXACTLY WHERE I PUT IT.

# 6. Study Smart

Okay, so you've remembered to bring home everything you need from school. Now it's time to do your homework. If you're like many kids, the idea of homework probably isn't all that exciting. But getting it done doesn't have to be the chore it might seem. You can try these tips to make studying go more smoothly.

**Get in a homework routine.** It's important to do homework at the same time each day. Afternoon is usually best. Take a break after school to move around a bit and have a snack. Then get started. If you have school activities in the afternoon, you might have to wait to do homework until after dinner. Whenever the best time is for you, try to do it at a regular time. It's a lot easier to get studying done when it's part of your normal routine.

**QUICK TIP:**

If you don't have any homework, you might use your study time to read, complete workbooks, learn vocabulary words, go through study cards, or work on the computer.

**Use a stopwatch.** Set a goal to study for a certain period of time and stick with it. You can use a stopwatch to time yourself. For example, if you want to study science for fifteen minutes, start the stopwatch when you begin studying. If you stop studying for any reason, stop the stopwatch. Start it again when you return to studying science. This can help you stay on task and keep track of how much time you're actually studying.

**Have a study-friendly space.** The place where you do homework should be quiet and well lit. It can be helpful to have a special study desk or table that you don't use for anything else. When you're seated at it, you'll know it's time to study. On your desk or table, have only the homework you're doing right then. Keep all your study supplies handy—like in a desk drawer or basket. Good supplies to have include pencils, pens, a highlighter, paper, erasers, a ruler, a stopwatch, a stapler, paper clips, a dictionary, folders, a calculator, and tape.

**Keep down noise and interruptions.** Turn off all cell phones, televisions, and radios in your study area. Some kids with ADHD *do* like to listen to calming music from a CD to block out small noises. This is okay as long as your parent approves. Ask your friends to respect your homework time by not calling when you're studying. If you're working on the computer, keep email and instant messaging programs closed so you're not distracted.

**Take breaks.** Remember to take a short break every twenty minutes or so. You might use breaks to get a drink of water, have a snack, or do some stretches. If you're using a stopwatch, be sure to stop it during breaks so you know how much time you're actually studying.

**Have a "study buddy."** Ask your teacher to find another student in your class who can help. You can call, email, or work with this person if you get stuck with parts of your homework. Your study buddy may sit next to you and help you with problems that come up in class.

**Do the easiest work first.** If some of your homework is hard and some is easy, do the easy parts first. When you get to the parts that are harder for you, remember this rule: If you can't figure something out in two minutes, stop trying and move on to other homework. When you feel ready to try the hard problems again, go ahead. If you still can't figure out how to do something after two minutes, get the help of a parent, study buddy, or teacher.

## QUICK TIP:

You also might be able to remember information better if you're moving as you learn it. You might try walking around your study area as you read facts that will be on a test.

**Say it, see it, touch it.** It can be easier to remember things if you say them out loud when you see them. Using your fingers to "write" information also can help. For example, to learn a new spelling word you could trace the letters on your desk or arm. Look at your hand as you trace the letters. Say the letters out loud.

**Use study cards.** Write class notes and test information on small note cards and study them to get ready for tests. You can write questions on one side of the cards and answers on the other. When you're studying, you might put the cards into two piles—one for those things you've learned and one for those you need more practice on.

**Be prepared for tests.** Go to sleep early the night before a test and review early on the morning of the test. Go through your study cards in the morning before going to school. Be sure to have a really good breakfast. Having a snack of cheese or nuts also is a good idea before tests.

**QUICK TIP:**
Chapter 4 has many other foods that are good for ADHD.

**Remember to bring homework back to school.** Some kids with ADHD work very hard to do their homework, then forget to take it back to school the next day. To avoid this problem, put finished assignments in the homework pocket folder of your binder. Then put your binder in your backpack. To remember your backpack, you could put it next to your door so you can't miss it the next morning.

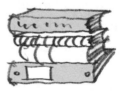

# CHAPTER 6 QUIZ

Are teachers from outer space? What's an IEP? How can you stay organized? See if you can answer these and other questions on the quiz below. The answers are upside down at the bottom of the page.

**1.** Tyrone has an IEP at school to help him succeed with ADHD. What does IEP stand for?

A. **I**cky **E**ctoplasmic **P**roblem

B. **I**nteresting **E**ating **P**lan

C. **I**ndividualized **E**ducation **P**lan

**2.** Jacquie struggles with written reports. What can she do?

A. Pretend her hands don't work so she doesn't have to write or type.

B. Tell her teacher that reports get in the way of her social life.

C. Ask her teacher if she can do an oral presentation instead of a written report.

**3.** Teachers are:

A. Aliens from another planet.

B. Part of your ADHD team.

C. Undercover spies who are trying to get kids in trouble.

**4.** Zach often forgets an assignments and loses worksheets. What is the best plan for Zach?

A. Use a binder and an assignment notebook to stay organized.

B. Tell his teacher that he is allergic to schoolwork.

C. Buy a personal robot assistant that can help him stay organized.

**Answers:** 1. C. 2. C. 3. B. 4. A. (Although a personal robot assistant also would be awesome!)

# Seven Ways to Make and Keep Friends

One of the best parts of life is spending time with friends. It's great to hang out with others and do fun activities. But sometimes it's a challenge for kids with ADHD to make and keep friends. Other kids often don't know a lot about ADHD. Maybe they don't respond to you the way you'd like them to.

If you want to change the way other kids think about you, keep reading. This chapter has some tips to help you be a good friend and get along better with other kids. How can you begin? Here's a hint: It all starts with you.

# I. Feel Good About Yourself

You might be thinking, "What does feeling good about myself have to do with other kids?" The answer is *a lot!* When you believe that you are an important and interesting person, other kids are more likely to think so, too.

> What are you good at? What positive qualities do you have? Write down some of the great things about you. Keep the list handy as a ready reminder of how great you are.

How can you feel good about yourself? Take a minute to remember all of the great things about you. You have many unique abilities and qualities. When you take time to remember what they are, you can get a boost in confidence. And when you're confident in who you are, you're likely to get a better reaction from other kids.

# 2. Use Polite and Kind Words

A lot of how you get along with others depends on being polite and kind. Think about it for a second. You probably don't want to be friends with people who are mean to you or boss you around. Other kids don't want to be around those people either. That's why it's important to speak nicely to others and use polite words like "please," "thank you," and "excuse me." If you do or say something that's unkind, you can apologize. Try saying something like, "I'm sorry. I shouldn't have said that. Please forgive me."

Another great way to show kindness is to compliment others. Give a big smile and say, "That was a great play you made in the field today" or "Nice shirt! Where did you get it?" Compliments are great because they show other kids that you like and enjoy being with them.

## CHECK THIS OUT:

*Social Smarts: Manners for Today's Kids* by **Carol Barkin.** This book has ideas for putting your best foot forward in all kinds of situations—including when you're out with friends.

# 3. Listen and Show You Care

How do you feel when people don't listen to you? Or when people interrupt you to say something they're thinking? You probably don't like it. You want people to listen to what *you* have to say. A huge part of being a good friend is listening well. Here's the secret to listening: Look people in the eye as they speak and don't say anything until they finish talking.

You also can show that you care about how others feel. For example, if friends share good news with you, show them you understand how happy they are. Try saying something like, "That's great! You must be really glad!" Another way to show you care is by listening closely when a friend wants to talk about problems or tough times that are happening. You might say something like, "That must be really hard to deal with." If you've been in a similar situation, maybe you can offer a friend some advice.

Want one more way to show that you care? Ask questions. For example, if a classmate is in the school band, you might ask when the band performs or what songs it plays. If you don't know much about someone, you might ask something simple like, "Did you see that great BMX show on TV last night?" If people don't know what you're talking about, you might ask them what shows *they* like. When you ask people about themselves, the chances go up that you'll find things you both like. Then you'll have more to talk about together.

**LISA**  "Whoa!!! Great back handspring!" Lisa said. It was lunch period and she was in the commons area. The new girl in Lisa's class was doing a few gymnastics moves on the lawn. Lisa was impressed. "Where did you learn to do jumps like that?" she asked. The tumbling girl stopped and came over to where Lisa was sitting. "My old school," she said. "I had a great coach there." Lisa stood up and introduced herself. The new girl told Lisa her name was Fatimah. Lisa had a hundred questions for Fatimah. She wanted to know about Fatimah's home country, her family life, why she had moved. Fatimah was happy to talk. For a few weeks she'd felt pretty alone in the new school. Lisa listened closely to what Fatimah had to say. "It must be hard to be in a new school," Lisa said. "Not to worry! You have a friend in me!" ∎

# 4. Take Turns and Share

Have you ever really liked something that someone else was playing with and wanted to give it a try? Maybe the person it belonged to wouldn't let you have a turn. Did you get upset? Other kids also get frustrated when people don't share. If you're right in the middle of using something that someone wants to see, you can say something like, "I'm using this right now, but you can use it when I'm done."

Sharing doesn't have to do only with games, toys, or other objects. You also can share responsibility. If you're working on a class project with others, for example, you'll want to cooperate and make sure everyone has a chance to give ideas and help out. People don't like when one person makes all the decisions and bosses others around. That's why it's important to let everyone participate. Go further by complimenting them in front of the group. The same goes for when you're on a team. Encourage others and be a good sport whether your team wins or loses. Games are a lot more fun when you play for enjoyment.

# 5. Try New Activities

It's hard to make friends sitting alone at home or standing by yourself on the playground. It can be a lot more fun to take part in activities at your school or in your neighborhood. Joining in games and activities shows other kids that you enjoy spending time with them and want to be friends. If you feel shy or nervous, you might join a game by saying something like, "Hey, this looks like a fun game. Mind if I play?" Even if there's no room for you in that game, you might be able to play in the next one.

At school, you can try sports like soccer, gymnastics, baseball, tennis, track, and volleyball. You might also like other activities—like band, drama, and choir. These activities can be some of the most fun parts of school. And doing fun things with others is a great way to strengthen friendships.

School isn't the only place where you can join in activities. You also can meet others doing fun things in your neighborhood. Try places like the YMCA, park leagues, clubs, scouts, and religious youth groups. Maybe you'd like to take a community class—for example, dance, exercise, martial arts, or music classes.

## CHECK THESE OUT:

 Here are four great organizations kids can join to have fun, learn important skills, and make more friends. Visit their Web sites to find opportunities in your area.

**Boys and Girls Clubs of America (www.bgca.org)**
**Boy Scouts of America (www.scouting.org)**
**Girl Scouts of America (www.girlscouts.org)**
**Campfire USA (www.campfire.org)**

# 6. Offer to Help Others

One great way to connect with others is to help them in different ways. When you help people, you show you care about them. They can feel glad to know you are a good friend to them. There are tons of ways you can help out others. For example, you might know a lot about a certain kind of math and help a classmate learn how to do it. If you're an expert on computers, you can show others how to do fun things with different programs.

**QUICK TIP:**

When you volunteer at school and in your neighborhood, you'll be working together with other kids (and adults) who can become your friends.

You might also pitch in at school or volunteer in the community. For example, you could sign up to work on events the school is planning—like a school carnival or science program. In your neighborhood, you could volunteer for programs that keep the community clean or do yardwork for people who need help.

# 7. Solve Conflicts Peacefully

Friends don't always agree on everything—even best friends who've known each other for a long time. Disagreements can come up between you and your friends, too. Maybe you don't agree about which game to play or whether you were safe at home plate. During conflicts, it helps to stay calm and talk things out.

When you're talking, don't blame other people for problems that come up. This usually just makes people more upset. A good way to avoid blaming is to use **I-MESSAGES**. What are I-messages? They're handy, conflict-solving sentences that use the words "I," "me," and "my." When you use these messages, you won't blame others because you are talking about *your* feelings.

| Blaming: | I-Messages: |
|---|---|
| *"You always decide what game we play."* | *"I'd like to choose the game we play sometimes."* |
| "You're wrong. There's no way that's a touchdown." | "I don't think that was a touchdown." |
| *"You never listen to my ideas on projects."* | *"I want us to use some of my ideas on the project, too."* |
| "That was a really crummy thing you did back there." | "I don't think it was right to do that." |

I-messages can also come in handy when other people are teasing you or calling you names. People who tease you are usually trying to get a reaction out of you. Maybe they want you to do or say something back to them so you get in trouble. Instead of fighting, yelling, or teasing back, you can stay calm and use I-messages to deal with the conflict. When you use I-messages, you don't give others the satisfaction of having power over your behavior.

**I-Messages for Dealing with Teasing:**

*"I don't like being called names."*

"I don't want to fight."

*"I don't think you're treating me with respect."*

"My feelings are hurt and I'd like an apology."

What if using I-messages doesn't work to stop someone from bothering or teasing you? Try these smart ways to end teasing.

**1.** Ignore the person.

**2.** Walk away.

**3.** Smile at the person and say that the teasing doesn't bother you.

**4.** Get an adult to help you.

## CHECK THESE OUT:

 ***Simon's Hook* by Karen Burnett.** Simon has a problem. People often tease him and try to make him react in bad ways. Will Simon catch on to this game and learn to deal with mean people in a better way?

 ***Speak Up and Get Along!* by Scott Cooper.** This book has 21 tools you can use to stand up for yourself, stop teasing, make friends, and feel good about yourself.

# CHAPTER 7 QUIZ

How much have you learned about getting along with other kids? Take this quiz to find out. Answers for the quiz are upside down at the bottom of the page.

**1.** Which of these are polite words?

   A. please, thank you, you're welcome, excuse me, I'm sorry

   B. pow, zoinks, shazam, razzamatazz, bonkers

   C. quiet on the set, lights, camera, action, cut

**2.** When someone's talking, it's best to:

   A. Plug your ears, close your eyes, and hum to yourself.

   B. Interrupt the person with your own story.

   C. Look the person in the eye and stay quiet until he or she is done speaking.

**3.** Jackson wants to be friends with Laurie, the new girl at school. What should he do?

   A. Introduce himself and ask Laurie about herself.

   B. Make faces at Laurie.

   C. Start bragging to Laurie about how he's the boss of the school.

**4.** Diane is playing soccer with a big group of kids. Which of these is a good thing she can do as she plays?

   A. Shout, "I'm #1! I'm #1!" whenever she makes a good play.

   B. Compliment others on nice plays they make on the field.

   C. Hog the ball whenever she gets it so that no one else can help score a goal.

**Answers:** 1. A. 2. C. 3. A. 4. B.

# CHAPTER 8

# Eight Ways to Deal with Strong Feelings

"I have a hard time controlling anger. Stuff builds up inside me until I explode."

"Keeping up in class is tough. I worry about school all the time."

"Sometimes it seems like I can't do anything right."

Being a kid with ADHD is not always easy. Parents and teachers probably expect a lot from you. It might seem as if you have to work really, really hard to do well. Maybe you feel like there's no room for you to make a mistake—that people will get angry if you're not perfect. When the pressure is on, it can be easy for you to feel super stressed.

Stress isn't the only strong feeling kids with ADHD might have. Many kids with ADHD also have trouble controlling anger. When these kids get angry, they might do or say things that hurt others. Other kids with ADHD may not have problems with anger, but instead they feel anxious or sad a lot of the time. Some are sad so often that they become **depressed.** These kids often feel as if there is nothing they can do to make things better.

What if you feel very sad or upset and there's no one around to talk with *right now?* Call the Nineline (1-800-999-9999). It's a hotline where people are ready to talk with you about your feelings anytime of day or night.

Feeling angry, sad, or stressed sometimes is normal. You can use ideas from this chapter to help you calm down and feel better. But if you feel any of these strong feelings *a lot* of the time, it's important to talk with a trusted parent, counselor, or another professional you see. These people can help you manage your feelings when things seem out of control.

# 1. Use Your Own Traffic Light

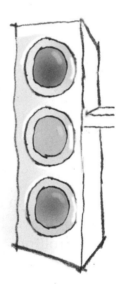

Strong feelings like anger are a natural part of life for everyone. How you deal with strong feelings is what's important. How can you manage strong feelings without doing something you'll regret later? One way is to imagine that you have your own traffic light. Traffic lights, of course, have three colors to help manage vehicles on the road: green for go, yellow for slow down, and red for stop. When you're in tough situations, you can use your traffic light to manage your actions by figuring out what color—green, yellow, or red—describes how you feel.

**Green light means go.** If you're feeling safe and calm in a situation, think **GREEN:** "I can stay here. It's okay for me to keep doing what I'm doing."

**Yellow light means slow down and be careful.** If you feel yourself getting upset about something, think

**YELLOW:** "I should be careful here. I could get angry or lose control. It's okay for me to stay for now, but if I get more upset I'll have to leave this situation." As you try to stay calm, you might take deep breaths and repeat to yourself, "I can stay in control."

**Red light means stop.** If you are upset or angry, think **RED:** "I should stop being here. I'm angry now. I need to put my hands in my pockets, zip my lip, and leave."

## CHECK THIS OUT:

***Don't Rant and Rave on Wednesdays* by Alfred Moser.** This fun book explains how anger affects people and offers safe ways to deal with it. Check it out for ways to change from mad to glad in no time.

# 2. Take Care Of Yourself

Taking care of yourself is a really great way to keep feelings under control. When you eat well and get enough sleep, your body and brain are able to work together well. You'll be in a better mood and can feel more in control of what you do.

Chapter 4 has many examples of foods that can help you feel your best. Sleep also is very important. Kids with ADHD usually feel best with at least nine hours. Without that much, you might start to feel grumpy and annoyed. If you're already in a bad mood, the smallest conflict can make you feel as if you're going to blow up.

# 3. Get Your Move On

Another great way to take care of yourself is to get plenty of exercise. Not only will you stay fit and healthy, but you'll also feel better. Why? When you're active, your body releases *endorphins*—natural chemicals that make your body feel good.

Exercise also can help for those times when you feel upset. When you're active, you use up energy—energy that could come out in negative ways.

> **A Few Ways to Get Your Move On**
> **(Can you think of others?)**
>
> inline skating • hiking • gymnastics • baseball • wakeboarding • volleyball • ice skating • jumping rope • skateboarding • dancing • running • biking • football • basketball • paintball • swimming • hockey • skiing • snowboarding

# 4. Use Breathing and Muscle Relaxation Exercises

If you're feeling stressed, angry, or sad, try doing breathing or muscle relaxation exercises. These exercises are great ways to calm down when you feel like things are spinning out of control. Your first step is to find a quiet place where you can be alone. To do a breathing exercise, sit or lie down. If you're sitting, sit up straight with your feet flat on the floor. If you're lying down, lie on your back and put pillows under your neck and knees. When you're in the position you like, take ten long, slow, deep breaths.

As you breathe, count down from ten or repeat positive messages to yourself. (For example, think "relax" when you breathe in and "I'm in control" when you breathe out.) You might also want to think of a place that makes you feel calm—like a beach, a relative's house, or some other place you like. Imagine that you are at that place. If it helps, you can look at a picture of the place as you do your breathing exercise.

"10... 9..."

**QUICK TIP:**

Listening to soft music as you do breathing and muscle relaxation exercises also can help. Some CDs have relaxing sounds or instructions for doing exercises.

You might also want to try a muscle relaxation exercise. Lie down with pillows under your neck and legs. One at a time, make your muscles go tight, then loose. Start with the muscles in your feet and move up your body—to your legs, stomach, chest, arms, neck, and head. Then do the same thing from your head down to your toes. As you tighten and loosen your muscles, you might repeat positive messages to yourself or think of a place where you feel calm.

# 5. Get Creative

One great way to handle strong feelings is to write about them. You might write in a journal or make up poems about something that's bothering you. If writing isn't your thing, you could create art that shows how you feel. If you're upset, it can help to draw a picture of a time or place you felt calm and happy. Writing and drawing can help you understand your feelings and get you thinking about ways to make things better.

Drawing and writing are not the only creative ways to feel better when something is bothering you. You might also work on a hobby that you have—like gardening or some other activity you enjoy. Hobbies are great ways to take your mind off things that might be bothering you. When you come back to problems later, it will be with a fresh outlook.

---

**A Few Ways to Get Creative**
**(Can you think of others?)**

write poetry or stories • sing or play an instrument • create your own comic book • make a scrapbook • make jewelry • build a model • bake a cake • invent a game • work on a puzzle • knit or crochet • do woodwork • write a computer program • make a collage • draw or paint a picture

# 6. Hang Out with a Friend

Friends are important. They can offer you support when things don't seem to be going your way. Talking with someone can help you get a grip on feelings. A friend might also have a solution to a problem that's bothering you.

Of course, friends also are great for fun. Playing a game or doing something else you like can take your mind off what's upsetting you. Having a laugh with friends also is a great way to relieve stress. You and a friend might want to watch a funny TV show or movie together, tell jokes, or do something else that gives you both a chuckle. Chances are, you'll feel better in no time!

# 7. Talk with an Adult

Just as talking with friends can help you deal with strong feelings, so can speaking with an adult. When you're upset or have a problem, ask a parent, counselor, or another adult you trust to have a chat.

NEXT TIME YOU MIGHT TELL THE TEACHER WHEN MIKE TEASES YOU.

You might want to talk about how you feel—or get advice on how to deal with a situation. Most adults have been through things that you're experiencing. They might tell you how they handled tough spots.

## CHECK THIS OUT:

***What to Do When You're Sad & Lonely* by James J. Crist.** This book has ideas that can help you feel better if you have the blues or are feeling really down.

Try to talk with adults regularly about ADHD challenges. You might want to do this at the same time each day—maybe at supper or before bed. Bring up anything that you had a hard time with and listen to the ideas adults have to make things go better.

# 8. Work on ADHD Challenges

A really great way to feel good about yourself and more in control of your ADHD is to work on the things that are hard for you. Work with parents and other adults to set goals and face challenges. You can use this book along the way—including the progress chart on page 106. When you work on the things that are hard for you, you can have more success at home and school. Strong, hard-to-control feelings can come on less often. And you can be proud of the progress you are making on your ADHD.

# A Final Word

You've made it to the end of this book! I hope it has helped you face some of the challenges ADHD causes for you. Remember to stay positive and believe in yourself as you work on things that are hard for you. You're a special kid with a lot of potential!

# My Progress Chart

This form can help you work on ADHD challenges. List up to three goals you have for handling ADHD traits. Then, write in a score for how you've done for each day of the week. Scores are:

0 – I didn't work on my goal.
1 – I made a little progress toward my goal.
2 – I made a lot of progress toward my goal.
3 – I accomplished my goal.

## Goal 1: _____

| Sunday | Monday | Tuesday | Wednesday | Thursday | Friday | Saturday |
|--------|--------|---------|-----------|----------|--------|----------|
|        |        |         |           |          |        |          |

Notes: _____

_____

## Goal 2: _____

| Sunday | Monday | Tuesday | Wednesday | Thursday | Friday | Saturday |
|--------|--------|---------|-----------|----------|--------|----------|
|        |        |         |           |          |        |          |

Notes: _____

_____

## Goal 3: _____

| Sunday | Monday | Tuesday | Wednesday | Thursday | Friday | Saturday |
|--------|--------|---------|-----------|----------|--------|----------|
|        |        |         |           |          |        |          |

Notes: _____

_____

# CHAPTER 8 QUIZ

Now that you're in the know about dealing with strong feelings, you can take this quiz. Answers to the quiz are upside down at the bottom of the page. Don't stress out—it's easy!

**1.** A group of kids is teasing Mike and he feels ready to blow up like a volcano. What can he do to get out of the situation before he explodes?

   A. Activate the helicopter blades that are hidden in his hat and fly away.

   B. Pull the cord on his backpack that turns it into a go-cart he can race away in.

   C. Follow his imaginary traffic light and walk away.

**2.** Which of these is a great way to relax?

   A. Run around the neighborhood screaming loudly.

   B. Take a high school algebra exam—just for fun!

   C. Do breathing and muscle relaxation exercises.

**3.** Eliza feels worried and anxious almost all of the time. What should she do?

   A. Talk with a parent or another trusted adult about how she feels.

   B. Stay in bed all day long.

   C. Eat two boxes of chocolate donuts.

**4.** How can working on ADHD challenges help you feel better about yourself and deal with strong feelings?

   A. Working on challenges will teleport you to another galaxy.

   B. Taking on challenges can help you feel good about progress you are making with your ADHD.

   C. Figuring out challenges will help you to discover the mysteries of the earth.

**Answers:** 1. C. (Although having a personal helicopter would be pretty great!) 2. C. 3. A. 4. B.

# GLOSSARY

This part of the book explains the words in **bold** type that you have read in the chapters.

**ADD (attention deficit disorder):** A label sometimes given to people when differences in the way their brains work make it hard for them to pay attention. The label used most often by professionals is "ADHD, Inattentive type."

**ADHD (attention deficit hyperactivity disorder):** A label people are given when differences in the way their brains work make it hard for them to pay attention or stay still. There are three types of ADHD.

**ADHD coach:** A person who helps kids with ADHD face the challenges ADHD creates for them and their families.

**allergens:** Substances in the air or in food that can cause bad reactions in people's bodies. Common allergens are found in dust and some foods.

**BD (behavior disorder):** A label given to kids who have trouble showing good behavior. ED, EBD, SED, or other labels sometimes are used for these kids.

**carbohydrates:** Sugars and starches found in breads, cereals, and vegetables.

**counselor:** A professional who talks with people about their feelings and tries to help them feel better.

**depressed:** Feeling very sad or hopeless for long periods of time.

**family counselor:** A professional who talks with families and gives advice for making things go better at home.

**hyperactive:** An ADHD trait that means it's hard to stay still or quiet.

**IDEA (Individuals with Disabilities Education Act):** A law that makes sure schools in the United States teach kids with special needs in the ways they learn best.

**IEP (Individualized Education Plan):** A plan that lists the learning needs of kids with LD (learning differences) and explains ways teachers can help them succeed at school. IDEA requires that kids in special education have IEPs.

**impulsive:** This ADHD trait means doing or saying things too quickly without thinking enough about them.

**inattentive:** This ADHD trait means having a hard time paying attention.

**indecisive:** This ADHD trait means that it takes a long time to make decisions.

**LD (learning differences):** A label given to kids who learn in ways different than most people.

**nervous system:** A system of nerves that carries messages around the body. For example, if you're trying to be still, the brain will send the message "be still" to the other parts of your body using the nervous system.

**neurologist:** A doctor who understands how the human brain works and who is an expert on the nervous system.

**nutrients:** Parts of food that give the body and brain energy and help them stay healthy.

**nutritionist:** A person who is an expert on food and how it helps our bodies.

**occupational therapist:** A professional who knows a lot about human senses. This expert helps kids with ADHD by teaching them helpful body exercises.

**pediatrician:** A doctor who knows a lot about how to help kids stay healthy.

**physician:** This is another word for *doctor.* Physicians go to medical school to understand how the human body works so they can help people stay healthy.

**proteins:** Liquids inside your brain and body that help you stay still and pay attention.

**preservatives:** Chemicals used to keep food from spoiling. Foods with lots of preservatives can be bad for kids with ADHD.

**psychiatrist:** A professional who knows a lot about how people think and act. Psychiatrists talk with people about their feelings and can prescribe medication to help them feel better.

**psychologist:** A professional who knows a lot about how people think and act. Psychologists talk with people about their feelings and try to help them feel better.

**resource room (or resource class):** A place at school where kids with LD (learning differences) go to get extra help.

**resource teacher:** A teacher who has special training to help students with LD (learning differences) study and learn.

**side effects:** Ways that medicines affect people that do not help them feel better.

**social worker:** A professional who talks with families and gives advice for making things go better at home.

**special education (or special ed):** Classes and learning opportunities for kids who have LD (learning differences).

**superfoods:** Foods that have many of the nutrients your body and brain need to stay healthy and strong.

**supplements:** Capsules, liquids, and tablets that help provide you with the nutrients your body and brain need to work well.

**traits:** Different ways people think, act, and feel. Traits affect how people do things and get along with others.

# A NOTE TO PARENTS, TEACHERS, AND COUNSELORS

ADHD can be challenging—but you and the young person reading this book know that. This resource is intended to help kids understand ADHD and give them effective ways they can manage it. Included are strategies and activities readers can use to improve behavior, organization, social skills, and academic performance.

You probably realize your important role in the life of the child reading this book. If you are a teacher or counselor, it's you who can help children modify problem behaviors, succeed in school, and get along with peers. If you are a parent, it is up to you to ensure your child is getting appropriate help in school, clinical, and counseling settings. It's you who must monitor medication's effectiveness (if it is being used), provide an ADHD-friendly diet, and support your child in other innumerable ways.

Following is a summary of the book's chapters along with information and ideas you can use to best help kids as they read. You likely will want to discuss ideas from the book with any professionals a child works with.

If you are wondering why the label ADD is not more prominent, it is because the American Psychiatric Association (APA) uses only the term ADHD—even when hyperactivity is not present. The condition commonly referred to as ADD is diagnosed as "ADHD, Inattentive type."

## Introduction

The Introduction offers an overview of some of the challenges kids with ADHD face—and how this book can help them improve in areas they struggle with. Readers are encouraged to share the book with parents, counselors, and other adults to work on ADHD challenges together.

## Chapter 1: What Is ADHD?

Readers learn about the ADHD label in Chapter 1. The cardinal traits of ADHD are hyperactivity, inattentiveness, impulsivity, and indecisiveness. Kids with ADHD usually demonstrate at least two of these traits at home and school. The chapter goes over the three different diagnostic types of ADHD. An activity is included that children can complete with adults to figure out the label that best describes them. Professionals who work with children will be able to shed additional insight on labeling issues.

## Chapter 2:  Make Each Day Go Better

Chapter 2 has three tools children can use to meet ADHD challenges. The first is a positive attitude. Readers learn that instead of feeling badly about problems related to behavior, school, and relationships, they can be positive about their potential to succeed. The KITE decision-making tool is offered as a method to help kids come up with positive actions for times when they're upset or unsure what to do. Finally, the LEAP tool helps young people realize that we all make mistakes, but that we can learn from them and keep from making the same ones in the future.

## Chapter 3: Getting Help for ADHD

Being labeled ADHD can be a confusing time for young people (and their families). This chapter goes over what happens during and after diagnosis. The goal is to help kids become active participants in the treatment process. The chapter outlines different ways medical, psychological, and counseling professionals help manage ADHD. Included in this discussion is medication. The majority of young people with ADHD—about three out of four—take a pharmaceutical at some point to address ADHD symptoms. Medication is serious business. Carefully review with children the indicators of successful medication treatment, as well as side effects. The most common reason medication treatment fails is that the dosage is incorrect. You can download a free dosage-finding form from www.add-plus.com as well as other forms that can be useful when working with professionals.

## Chapter 4: Eating the Right Food

Research is now verifying what common sense indicates: If you eat the nutrients the brain needs, your brain works better. If you don't give your brain the nutrition it needs, it doesn't work very well. These trends are magnified when a person has ADHD. Chapter 4 has dietary recommendations that can help keep the brain functioning highly. You may wish to work with a nutritionist or pediatrician to ensure your child is getting the very best in nutrition. Kids are encouraged to be active participants in maintaining an ADHD-friendly diet. As much as possible, family diets and routines should facilitate this participation.

In recent years there has been a considerable increase in the number and scientific rigor of studies appearing in professional journals regarding nutritional factors and toxic chemical exposure as factors in ADHD. More information, documentation, and reviews of the current scientific evidence on nutritional and toxic chemical exposure factors are available at www.add-plus.com.

## Chapter 5: Life on the Home Front

Families with children who have ADHD often experience more conflict than families that do not. Chapter 5 provides practical suggestions children can use to improve family relationships and overcome common challenges that surface during daily routines.

## Chapter 6: Six Ways to Succeed at School

The majority of kids with ADHD have one or more significant areas of academic difficulty. The most common complaint they make to school counselors is that they can't keep up with the work pressure. Nearly half of all young people with ADHD have at least one learning difference. This chapter explains how schools are required to provide for kids who have special needs. Also included are ideas for working well with teachers and tips for staying calm, focused, and organized in the classroom. It's important that parents, school officials, and other professionals work together to meet children's educational needs.

## Chapter 7: Seven Ways to Make and Keep Friends

One of the most commonly expressed concerns by children with ADHD is that they don't have enough friends. Many children with ADHD have trouble demonstrating basic social skills. As a result, they often are teased, ignored, or ostracized by peers. Many children with ADHD also are quick to become angry—conflicts often culminate in verbal arguments or physical fighting. This chapter reinforces important social skills and offers constructive ways to handle conflicts. Proper socialization is a critical issue for kids with ADHD; adults working with these young people should make social skills development a point of emphasis.

## Chapter 8: Eight Ways to Deal with Strong Feelings

The majority of hyperactive children have significant anger control problems. Those without hyperactivity (ADHD, Inattentive type) often are additionally diagnosed with anxiety or depression. Chapter 8 gives readers ideas for handling strong feelings like anger, stress, and sadness. It's encouraged throughout that children talk with adults they trust. Please make sure that you are available for children and remember to take their feelings seriously.

More detailed information on ADHD can be found in many available resources for parents, teachers, counselors, and other professionals. You can find a listing of some of these resources at www.add-plus.com and www.freespirit.com.

# INDEX

# ABOUT THE AUTHOR

John F. Taylor, Ph.D., works with kids and families affected by ADD and ADHD. A psychologist in private practice, John has helped thousands of kids manage ADHD to get along better with others and succeed in school. He is the author of many books, articles, and other resources on ADD and  ADHD, including *Helping Your ADD Child* and *From Defiance to Cooperation.*

John also is the founder and president of ADD Plus, a company that offers resources and workshops to parents, educators, and other professionals. He is a frequent speaker at national and regional conferences on the topics of ADD and ADHD, mental health, and education. To learn more about speaking opportunities and additional materials by John, visit www.add-plus.com.

# Other Great Books from Free Spirit

## The Survival Guide for Kids with LD*
## *(Learning Differences)
Revised & Updated Edition
*by Gary Fisher, Ph.D., and Rhoda Cummings, Ed.D.*
This edition retains the best of the original: the warmth, affirmation, and solid information kids need to know they're smart and can learn, they just learn differently. It explains what LD means (and doesn't mean); describes the different kinds of LD; talks about what happens in LD programs; helps kids deal with their feelings; suggests ways to get along better in school and at home; and inspires them to set goals and plan for the future. For ages 8 & up.
*112 pp.; softcover; illust.; 6" x 9"*

## The Behavior Survival Guide for Kids
How to Make Good Choices and Stay Out of Trouble
*by Thomas McIntyre, Ph.D. (Dr. Mac)*
Up-to-date information, practical strategies, and sound advice for kids with diagnosed behavior problems (BD, ED, EBD) and those with general behavior problems—so they can help themselves. For ages 9–14.
*176 pp.; softcover; illust.; 7" x 9"*

## How to Take the GRRRR Out Of Anger
*by Elizabeth Verdick and Marjorie Lisovskis*
Kids need help learning how to manage their anger. Filled with solid information, sound advice, and humor, this book helps kids understand anger and how to handle it in healthy, positive ways. It guides them to understand that anger is a normal part of life, but violence is not acceptable. For ages 8–13.
*128 pp.; softcover; illust.; 5¹/₈" x 7"*

## Get Organized Without Losing It
*by Janet S. Fox*
Kids today have a lot to keep track of—and keep organized. Schoolwork, activities, chores, rooms, backpacks, lockers…and what about fun? Here's practical, humorous help for kids who want to manage their tasks, their time, and their stuff—without going overboard. Kids learn to conquer clutter, prioritize tasks, plan projects, stop procrastinating, and enjoy the benefits of being organized: less stress and more success. For ages 8–13.
*112 pp.; softcover; 2-color; illust.; 5¹/₈" x 7"*

*For pricing information, to place an order, or to request a free catalog, contact:*

**Free Spirit Publishing Inc.**
**217 Fifth Avenue North • Suite 200 • Minneapolis, MN 55401-1299**
**toll-free 800.735.7323 • local 612.338.2068 • fax 612.337.5050**
**help4kids@freespirit.com • www.freespirit.com**